EUROPE/AMERICA

8

Europe and America
Beyond 2000

EUROPE/AMERICA 8

Europe and America Beyond 2000

Pierre Hassner
David P. Calleo
Robert D. Hormats
Johan Jørgen Holst
Richard Perle
David Owen

Gregory F. Treverton, editor

Council on Foreign Relations Press
New York • London

COUNCIL ON FOREIGN RELATIONS BOOKS

Copyright © 1990 by the Council on Foreign Relations, Inc.
All rights reserved.
Printed in the United States of America

First published in hard cover by New York University press, Washington Square, New York, NY 10033

This book may not be reproduced, in whole or in part, in any form (beyond that copying permitted by Sections 107 and 108 of the U.S. Copyright Law and excerpts by reviewers for the public press), without written permission from the publishers. For information, write Publications Office, Council on Foreign Relations, 58 East 68th Street, New York, NY 10021.

Library of Congress Cataloguing-in-Publication Data

Europe and America beyond 2000/by Pierre Hassner . . . [et al.] ; Gregory F. Treverton, editor.
    p.   cm. —(Europe/America ; 8)
    Includes bibliographical references.
    ISBN 0-87609-057-9
    1. Europe—Foreign relations—United States. 2. United States—Foreign relations—Europe. 3. Twenty-first century—Forecasts.
I. Hassner, Pierre. II. Treverton, Gregory F. III. Series.
D1058.E866 1989
327.4073—dc20
                                      89-39694
                                       CIP

Contents

Acknowlegements

The editor would like to thank William Diebold, Charles Maier, Stanley Heginbotham, Robert Hunter, F. Stephen Larrabee, Stanley Sloan, Steven Szabo, and Samuel Wells for their assistance in planning and/or commenting on the manuscripts. He would also like to thank David Kellogg, Suzanne Hooper, Bob Goldsmith, and Steven Monde for their assistance in the production of this book.

Foreword

This volume represents a transition in the Council's Europe-America Project, for it both closes one phase and foreshadows the next. It closes a series of books, written by authors who were not only serious students of trans-Atlantic issues but also, in many cases, distinguished practitioners that took what might be called an "alliance management" perspective. They inquired into issues confronting the alliance or those visibly on the horizon—ranging from nuclear and conventional weapons to economics to high technology to Central America to South Africa. In each book in the series, the authors sought to highlight where Europeans and Americans agreed and differed, where their interests overlapped and where they diverged, asking how the two sides of the Atlantic might reconcile differences so as to increase the prospects for wise policy while minimizing the chances that disputes would damage the basic structure of the alliance. The volumes in the Europe-America series are listed on the back cover.

Now, however, as we look ahead the basic structure of postwar Europe and of the American connection to it seem in question, perhaps for the first time since World War II. The reasons are happy ones—"1992" and "Gorbachev," to read the headlines—but the outcome is uncertain. It thus seems critical in the next phase of the Project to inquire into underlying structures. The need for American engagement to balance Soviet military power in Europe; trans-Atlantic economic dealings as positive-sum, with disputes resolvable and to be dealt with in general apart from security; the special role of a divided Germany in a divided Europe: these have been the premises of the European-American alliance.

Over the next years the Project will ask whether events are undermining those premises and if so, what assumptions should replace them. This will mean looking across the implications of 1992 to the effects of Gorbachev on an unfreezing order in Europe; it will mean thinking through several turns of events and of politics in both East and West.

This volume, capping the previous phase of the Project, is a prelude to that enquiry. We have asked six seasoned analysts and statesmen to look from economics to security and to stretch their minds to the year 2000 and beyond, asking what the trans-Atlantic alliance will or should look like by then; Gregory Treverton's introduction seeks to sharpen points of agreement and difference, and to lay the chapters beside each other. The perspective of a decade and a half hence is short enough so that not everything changes but long enough so that much does; basic structures are not likely to have changed by then, but the fault-lines that might produce such changes should be apparent. The book is an agenda for thinking about the premises of the alliance and a guide to the Project's next steps.

This transition point is also a welcome one to note the efforts of Dr. Treverton and his predecessor as Project Director, Andrew Pierre, and their immediate colleagues, past and present, Moira Coughlin and Steven Monde. I also express my thanks to the Project's Advisory Group and its Vice-Chair, Robert Hormats.

Cyrus R. Vance

Europe and America
Beyond 2000

Introduction:
Looking Beyond 2000

Gregory F. Treverton

The year 2000, which we have been accustomed to as the target of long-range speculation, is not so far away. It is now just around the corner. And although 2000 is not so far away that everything will change between then and now, it is far enough away that some critical particulars will change.

Looking beyond 2000 thus means looking at underlying structures, not at outcomes that, in Richard Neustadt's phrase, "depend for their achievement on precise conjunctions of particular procedures, men and issues."[1] (Writing now and mindful of Mrs. Thatcher, Neustadt no doubt would add "and women"—and not just for the sake of good manners, if clumsy prose, in the last years of the 20th century.) Imagining changes over 20 years means thinking through not a single dramatic alteration, but rather the cumulative effects of two or three smaller bites of change.

It means looking through changes to left-of-center governments in major European states, the Federal Republic, and Britain, and perhaps through more than one turn of domestic politics. Similarly, it means contemplating the possibility of turns in Soviet politics. Gorbachev might lose power or, more likely, gradually lose his ability to implement his reform programs.

So, taking a perspective beyond 2000 means looking through immediate politics to ask about structures beneath, where change is slower. That is hard even for this distinguished group of authors; ask any of us to think a decade-plus hence, and we are likely to stretch our minds two years.

Premises of Alliance

The question that runs through all these chapters is whether events are undermining the premises of the trans-Atlantic alliance. Certainly, the "tectonic plates" that have supported the web of political and economic arrangements across the Atlantic are moving; as Pierre Hassner puts it: "Every period is by definition a period of transition, but some are more transitional than others." The movements can be described in shorthand as "Gorbachev" and "1992," and the connection between them. Do they call into question, for the first time in the postwar period, the premises of the trans-Atlantic alliance? Two of these have been explicit, three implicit:

• The threat from the Soviet Union required constructing a military alliance, involving—for the first time in U.S. history— a relatively permanent American entanglement in Europe. If, with Stalin in the Kremlin, that was the "right" risk-averse choice, although at the margin it may have played a role in confirming Soviet hostility and the division of Europe, will it continue to be the "right" choice?

• The implicit counterpart to this premise is that eastern Europe would not disrupt the status quo. The alliance, and the North Atlantic Treaty Organization (NATO) in particular, was just what the allies labeled it, purely defensive. If the postwar stability of Europe was constructed on the backs of the eastern Europeans, that was a shame. But once the Eisenhower administration's urgings to "roll back" proved empty, it was plain that the allies could do little save try to mitigate the worst effects of eastern Europe's plight. And so long as Moscow could sustain stability in the region without too great bloodshed, the costs of the stability could be ignored.

• The liberal international economic order of which the United States and western Europe are the center was created mostly before the alliance's security arrangements. It has been assumed that economic relations among the allies are basically cooperative: competition produces comparative advantage, and all gain. Thus, specific disputes could be managed without unraveling the basic alliance connection. On the whole they were. But will that continue?

• Less explicitly, those disputes have been manageable, presumably, in part because of the shared tug of the security imperative. Bureaucratically, security and economics have been dealt with as separate issues along separate tracks. Since those tracks have crossed only at the top of government, it has been possible to back away from controversial economic issues lest they damage the security relationship. The allies have been able to impose short-run economic losses on their domestic politics for the sake of perceived long-run political and security gains: so it is generally argued. Will that continue if the security link loses force?

• Finally, and hardest to discuss, the postwar status quo, including the trans-Atlantic alliance, implied that the division of Germany was permanent. Adenauer's Federal Republic accepted that fact in joining NATO. This, too, was a shame, one that West German politicians speechified about on Sundays. But this, too, was something the allies could do little about other than try to mitigate its worst effects.

The postwar European order, no one's idea, has turned out to be enduring.[2] It has served Europe well by dividing German power, and thus solving the problem with which the continent grappled unsuccessfully for a hundred years. It also has served the United States well, by ratifying the American presence in Europe. The status quo seems to have served the Soviet Union at least as well. By dividing German power, it diminished the threat; by dividing the continent as well as Germany, it conferred the Soviet Union leverage over the Federal Republic, justified a large Soviet military presence in eastern Europe, and provided some legitimacy for regimes in eastern Europe that would otherwise have been unacceptable long before now.

The Soviet Threat

The authors agree that nuclear weapons will continue to exist and, in Pierre Hassner's words, to "exert to some degree their double effect—potential destruction and actual restraint." Or in

David Calleo's: "New Soviet interventions in eastern Europe. . .
are not so improbable. . . . But in a nuclear world Western
armies are unlikely to march to the rescue." By the same token,
none of the contributors to this volume thinks that the nature of
East-West relations in Europe will be so transformed in roughly
a decade that NATO will pass away. Beyond that, however, the
disagreement is broad. The faultline does not divide Americans
from Europeans, for the two authors most skeptical of change
in the Soviet Union are one American, Richard Perle, and one
European, David Owen.

Richard Perle's chapter is exhortation, not projection. His
underlying theme is that for all the change, the need to counterbalance Soviet military power in Europe—and for NATO in
more or less its present form—will remain. His argument that if
European leaders had access to the same intelligence apprecia-
tions of Soviet military power as their American counterparts,
they would draw the same conclusions, is hard to credit. But it
is hard to argue with his charge that by not being frank with
their own people, NATO leaders have done a disservice to their
alliance and their democracies. If more is changing than Perle
assumes, the argument for candor is all the stronger.

David Owen's assessment of the Soviet Union leads him to
share Perle's skepticism about change. Economic reform has so
far failed, yet tanks continue to roll off the assembly lines at
their pre-Gorbachev pace. In the international realm, especially, the Soviet Union has changed course sharply in the past and
could do so again in the future. Accordingly, Owen's prescrip-
tions imply the management of a relatively constant alliance in
changing circumstances. He argues for selective modernization
of NATO's nuclear arsenal, and while he regards it as inevitable
that some American troops will be withdrawn from Europe, he
hopes the pressure can be managed by cuts in the range of
50,000–70,000, preferably done unilaterally.

In the end, however, despite his skepticism, Owen concludes
that Gorbachev represents "an opportunity that might not
recur for many decades." The allies should gamble on helping
him, but with strings. The trick will be to pull those strings
together, rather than competing against each other, not just for

trade, but also for favors. Uncoordinated, the allies have no influence; together, they have some influence, even if it is indirect.

Johan Holst focuses on the nuclear dilemma at the heart of the alliance. He shares the assumption that nuclear weapons will continue to exist, and he finds it impossible not to credit them with contributing to Europe's postwar stability. In looking forward, he draws on the distinction between general and specific deterrence. So long as East-West hostility was taken for granted, the focus was specific deterrence—how to affect specific decisions in a crisis. That resulted in a NATO nuclear posture that was "the result of military assessments of operational requirements for covering specific target structures," reflecting a "war-fighting perspective" that "will alienate Western societies, eroding support for prudent defense policies."

His prescription is akin to Owen's: fewer weapons, deployed farther from the front line, with fewer battlefield systems. He thinks such a shift will be all the more attractive if negotiated reductions in conventional forces reduce the asymmetries that have, after all, induced NATO to rely so heavily on nuclear weapons in the first place.

Holst also argues that, especially as the forward deployments of the United States are drawn down, both the link between the central front and the northern flank and the importance of naval power more generally will grow. The United States will return to its more familiar role as provider of "expeditionary" forces. Yet his analysis, like others in the collection, assumes that the shift can be made without upsetting the basic structure of the NATO alliance.

Old Stability, New Unpredictability

Pierre Hassner's chapter is the boldest inquiry into a changing future. For him, what has been the most predictable element of the international system—Marxism-Leninism—has become the most unpredictable, even if its ultimate demise still is a safe long-run bet. After periods in which America and Europe seemed on diverging courses with regard to the East, most recently in the late 1970s and the early 1980s, now it is the East itself that provides the most potential for instability.

Hassner identifies three possible scenarios for the next decade-plus, and he concentrates on the one he regards as most likely—the breakup of the "vertical security system" organized around the two superpowers. Instead he foresees "two parallel, horizontal security partnerships," one a strategic dialogue between the superpowers, the other a continental system based on the middle European powers. America and western Europe would remain close economically and culturally—Hassner foresees no "Fortress Europe"—but would drift apart militarily and politically.

At both levels, states would have more freedom of action. For the West, the possible losses would be two: the link between the continental and superpower system would be broken, leaving both NATO's notion of escalation and British and French nuclear forces more or less hanging. And, given geography, the Soviet Union would be more present than the United States in the continental system, the "common European house."

Furthermore, this scenario, while the most likely, depends on an improbably harmonious evolution in eastern Europe and the Soviet Union—just the evolution that, as Hassner notes, the first half of his chapter deems unlikely. Nor is it certain that if a blowup occurs, the pattern of responses across Europe and America will be as they have in the past. Among the paradoxes of the postwar division is that while it was frustratingly frozen, it provided some insulation of societies from each other. Not so now, a fact illustrated in different ways by the end to jamming of Western broadcasts in eastern Europe and the backlash against immigrants from the East in West Germany. If a blowup did not occur for a few years, the United States might then have turned enough from Europe to react with relative indifference, while "conversely, the greater involvement of western Europeans may result in greater concern, a concern not always entirely benevolent in nature."

It is this uncertainty that leads Hassner to cast his vote for "a priority on western Europe." Real cooperation can be "based only on balance, and only a western European power can be both a valid interlocutor for a powerful United States and Soviet Union, and an effective stabilizer if either or both enter a vagarious period. Between globalism and nationalism, between capitalist interdependence and a Soviet-inspired 'common European house,' an autonomous western Europe starts as a poor third. But it has a fighting chance. . . . And given the stakes, if it has a chance, it is worth a try."

The Impact of Economics

Have the economic premises of the trans-Atlantic alliance eroded? Will they? The answers of two Americans, Robert Hormats and David Calleo, are most sharply different, yet both authors are in their ways optimistic. And surprisingly, perhaps, in view of recent American concerns over 1992 and Fortress Europe, none of the authors, including Calleo, thinks that West-West trade disputes themselves will undermine the alliance.

Consider the history of trans-Atlantic disputes. In 1974, a year of floating exchange rates, the oil embargo, Kissinger's détente, and a looming recession, there were four areas of friction: money, agriculture, high-technology trade, and energy. By 1982 three of these four areas remained issues, with East-West trade replacing energy. In 1989 the list comprised only two issues, agriculture and high-tech trade, but the other two 1982 issues, monetary questions and East-West trade, were latent and could erupt at any time.

Energy remains a potentially divisive issue, perhaps the biggest such issue, but not for the next five years. World oil prices are still not back to their pre-1973 levels in real terms, but have declined sharply (at least until very recently). Hence, demand for energy, flat for fifteen years, is now growing at nearly the same rate as gross national product.

The continuity of the lists is arresting. Equally so is the fact that the 1989 one did not include the European Community's (EC) drive for economic integration. Indeed, of the issues on any list, 1992 was related only to one—high-technology trade—and then only indirectly. 1992 certainly was salient, and, as Hormats notes, it will present a tactical problem for the

Europeans, since they will be simultaneously negotiating with each other over 1992 and with the rest of the trading world in the Uruguay Round—and over many of the same issues in both places. Hormats and Hassner, though, stress that Fortress Europe is unlikely, although a host of nitty-gritty, technical problems will emerge in implementing 1992 as nations adjust to the directives.

The continuity suggests that the issues seem the same but change in form. Disagreements arise but are contained without disrupting the basic structure of the alliance. While economics is more salient now, it is not obvious that its domestic politics are more difficult to manage than they were twenty years ago. If interdependence is not always pleasant, it is becoming a fact of life. In 1969 bankers were awed when $4 billion moved into Deutsche Marks in two days; now, that much moves in an hour.

Hormats makes the argument for continuity most directly. He presents an explicitly optimistic outlook, one that shares Owen's assumption that the structure of the alliance will not, or at least need not, change dramatically. Hormats reaches that conclusion by concentrating on prospects for western Europe from an American perspective. He judges the process of tearing down internal barriers in Europe irreversible even if it proceeds by fits and starts. He is optimistic that by 2000, the United States and the EC will have set in place a framework for settling trade disputes in a less acrimonious way than now. By 2000, too, he anticipates less trans-Atlantic disagreement over trade with eastern Europe and the Soviet Union, for by then the course of reform will be clearer. Like Owen, he argues for matching the economic benefits for the East to the pace of reform.

For Hormats, just as the allies hold most of the economic chips, so is their position strong in the security realm, for the Eastern countries need to shift resources from military to civilian purposes. Thus, a conventional force treaty providing for sharply asymmetrical cuts on the part of the Warsaw Pact is possible. It could be followed by reductions in short-range nuclear weapons. With luck, also, by 2000 the United States, having passed through a period of retrenchment, will have reestablished a domestic consensus in support of its military engagement—conventional and nuclear—in Europe.

Economics and Security

However, the presumption of continuity in the management of economic issues among the allies can be questioned in several ways. Of these, the overarching if also the most elusive is asking what will ensue if the shared imperative of security diminishes. The answers to the question are unprovable because they are untestable; the inquiry posits discontinuity. It says that even in the absence of other discontinuities, future economic management would not follow past patterns because all the allies will see less need to suffer the pain in their domestic politics of sacrificing some specific, economic interests for the sake of the broader security tie. And the future is all the less likely to resemble the past because there are other discontinuities as well. Those might be grouped into four categories:

The issues themselves. If they are not individually more difficult, they may be more numerous and cumulatively harder to control. The 1992 process will throw up a series of issues akin to that over beef hormones in 1989. What if two or three such issues break loose at the same time? If each is manageable, even trivial, in its own terms, will the sequence be? On the whole, the authors of this volume say "yes."

American and European interests. These may have changed, or so it is argued for the United States, which is less powerful economically relative to its allies. This fact is a result of past success and thus should hardly be bemoaned. Yet, is the United States doing damage to itself by playing the game the same way when it is no longer dominant—are the policies of the past still right for the future?

Changes in domestic politics. Such changes, especially in the United States, may make specific issues harder to manage. Even if the same policies as in the past continue to be "right" by abstract calculations of national interest, that calculation may not be reflected by the body politic. If the United States is perceived as less dominant than it used to be, the appeals of special interests may be harder to resist.

Europeans, too, feel interdependence makes for vulnerability. They deeply resented the October 1987 American crash, which they regarded as the result of unwise American policies; likewise, they resent Japanese plants even as they seek them. Winners and losers within Europe after 1992 will bring different pressures on European governments in responding to economic concerns.

The "European" negotiating beast may change as well. The Single European Act strengthened Brussels vis-a-vis the national governments, especially by sanctioning majority votes for most issues. Practical politics has slowed the effect of the change. What could make for more change is the role of the European Parliament, where the hormone issue began. Though the parliament has no formal authority over the European budget, it is edging toward de facto controls. The beef hormone issue could be the beginning of a host of issues of reciprocal retaliation between Brussels and Washington.

Changes beyond western Europe and America. Managing West-West economics could become more perilous as a result of certain changes. For instance, eastern European and Soviet economic issues might become political-cultural issues that could drive a wedge between the United States and Europe, a risk noted throughout this book. In addition, eastern Europe will be more and more interested in membership in the European Community, either formally or de facto.

A second such change is the increase in global players. With a less dominant position in the world markets, America and Europe may not be able to resolve issues that arise in the international forum—with a growing number of participants, consensus on goals, or even on how to frame the questions, will diminish.

Third, and most important, it seems that the enormous increase in Japan's role must make for friction in European-

American economics; one of the "tectonic plates" in motion now is East-West relations, but the other is Japan's role. Japan-bashing is now in vogue in Europe. More to the point, the row over Nissans made in Britain seems a prelude to the debate over whether Nissans made in Tennessee are American or Japanese, assuming that the EC retains quotas on Japanese car imports even after 1992.

All these arguments about discontinuity have specific counters. Europe has long had to deal with regional disparities; those become sources of trans-Atlantic friction only if they are resolved by subsidizing the exports of poorer regions. In process terms, Europe may now have created machinery that rivals Washington in obscurity, complexity, and unpredictability. To the extent, however, that the changes make "Europe" a more cohesive bargainer, that can make bargaining for the United States easier—because there is only one partner—as well as harder—because that partner may be more powerful.

Japan has been a factor in London's financial world for two decades, so little about that is new. To the extent it is more prominent, that may drive Europe and America together more than apart; in that sense, the argument about semiconductors in the 1980s was an exception. (However, if Europe tries to discriminate against Japan, it will hit the United States too, since the GATT prohibits such singling out.) Similarly, the presence of more global actors may drive the two sides of the Atlantic alliance together; they are, for instance, closer on most Third World issues than they are on how to deal with eastern Europe.

Moreover, it may be a mistake to pose the issue as that of "economics versus security." For the United States, long-run economic interests may have paralleled long-run political ones. Both have indicated resistance to specific economic pleadings. Hence a natural alliance has formed between the State Department and the Council of Economic Advisors (CEA): what State wants for political reasons, CEA favors because it is inflation-fighting or antiprotectionist.

Calleo locates his argument in the realm of national interests and their connection to underlying structures, explicitly linking economics and security. His, like Hassner's, is an exploration of those structures. For him, the movement of the tectonic plates points to a "more plural geopolitical order." When he looks at the nuclear evolution treated by Holst, his conclusion is more dramatic: "The United States cannot continue to guarantee Europe's security. . . . This is not to say that the Atlantic alliance is doomed. If the United States can no longer be a hegemonic protector, it can certainly remain an ally."

Moreover, "this pluralist military logic seems all the more forceful because it runs parallel to broad trends in the world economy." In policy terms, the United States has settled into some "very bad habits"—reflected as the 1990s begin by its twin deficits. More historically, Calleo echoes the thesis widely attributed to Paul Kennedy in seeing America as running the risk of becoming a "'hegemon in decay,' an overstretched power that. . . undermines itself and breaks up the global system into competing protectionist blocs." However uncertain Gorbachev's tenure in the Soviet Union may be, a turn toward reaction there would not "eliminate the need for America's geopolitical consolidation and Europe's greater military self-sufficiency."

For America's allies in Europe, Calleo's prescription is "devolution," their assuming primary responsibility for their own defense. He is optimistic that they will, and can: "Europe's major states have never ceased to be concerned about their military security." The renewed momentum of the EC is grounds for optimism, for sustaining a security coalition should be easy by comparison with economic integration. Moreover, the most apocalyptic scenarios all assume no one, least of all the Europeans, has learned anything since the 1950s—for instance, about the dangers of West Germany looming too large in Europe's push eastward.

For Calleo, the ultimate question is whether "the liberal world economy can survive America's declining hegemony." If it can, western Europe can escape from America's abiding postwar fear—that it would be too weak and divided to balance Soviet power—and the Soviet Union can slowly be brought into the world system in a way that will signify "a much greater gain for the world than a loss for U.S.–European ties." If Hassner's uncertainty about events in the East leads him to bet, finally, on western European construction, and Hormats hopes, along with Owen, for a happy but gradual evolution of the status quo, Calleo is more optimistic still, sketching a "rebalancing" among Europe, America, and the Soviet Union.

The Center of Europe

The contributors to this volume underscore the importance of Europe's center, the two Germanies, but they are relatively circumspect in speculating about its future. That reflects more than politeness, for no doubt real change in the center of Europe is not in any case likely for the next two decades. The assumption is fair enough, but long before change occurs Europe's politics and that of the European-American alliance will be affected by the shadow of possibilities.

Events in eastern Europe are transfixing, but while they may disturb the continent's status quo, they become decisive only through their impact on central Europe—for which read "Germany." Germans can be forgiven for regarding the Americans or the French as obsessive about the "German question"—a point Calleo makes. "Reunification" is not on the agenda; while Federal German public opinion polls indicate overwhelming support for reunification in principle—only the Greens publicly disavow the idea—those same polls suggest that few West Germans think it is possible soon.[3]

Yet events *are* pushing forward questions about the role of the Germanies, especially of the Federal Republic and its connections to both its European and its American partners. The attractions of the 1992 process for eastern Europe are discussed throughout this book, and the authors, by emphasizing the need for coordinated Western economic policies toward the East, underscore the risk that the opening eastward will be a divisive scramble, not a coordinated EC effort, let alone an agreed European-American one. As the process advances, the fact that East Germany is a de facto EC member through its link to West Germany will become more salient. More generally, when eastern Europeans talk about economic connections with the "West," they mean, for all their ambivalence, the Federal Republic, even if the magnitudes are small by comparison to overall West German economic dealings.

For its part, the West German vision seems to be one of concentric circles: the EC after 1992 as a platform for increasing German links eastward, with NATO as a kind of European lever on American dealings with the Soviet Union. Calleo is hopeful about this vision: the "possibility of an eastern Europe dominated by German finance and industry would please none of Germany's neighbors—to the east or to the west." To believe it will come about is to believe that "no one has learned anything from Europe's past mistakes." At its center the vision is fuzzier, and it has to be, but for Calleo it amounts to the short-term goal of better conditions in East Germany and the long-term hope of confederation within "some broader pan-European system—a sort of extended European Community."

In the security realm, while some strategic theologians (myself included) thought the 1987 intermediate-range nuclear forces treaty was about the shape of Europe and the American connection to it, the Conventional Forces in Europe (CFE) talks seem to be about little else. Suppose, for instance, that over a decade or so, both sides reduce their personnel, major ground armaments, and aircraft to half the current NATO level. Short-range nuclear forces are eliminated or reduced to nominal levels. This would seem, politically, an outcome so happy as to be almost beyond conceiving except that, with Gorbachev, yesterday's wild speculation has a way of becoming tomorrow's conventional wisdom.

This outcome would signify major changes in Europe's landscape. NATO would be substantially denuclearized and thus, given its structure, de-Americanized. The threat of nuclear escalation in flexible response would be, as Hassner puts it, left hanging, as would the nuclear forces of Britain and France. If every nation's commitment of troops fell by half, the stationing of foreign troops in the Federal Republic would become, apart from the United States, a symbolic affair. And NATO would be in the midst of an open debate about doctrine, one especially sensitive for the West Germans.

Not all of this need be bad. NATO has changed doctrine before, as Holst notes. But it is a mistake to see the changes purely in military terms, as NATO's graceful decay in response to a declining threat, or as competitive decline between the West's incredible strategy and the East's unbelievable threat. The change is political. It is about the shape of Europe and, in particular, the Federal Republic's role.

The German-American dustup over short-range nuclear forces in 1989 was, in its own terms, important only to strategic theologians. But it did illustrate the shifting center of gravity in West German security politics. It had been customary, especially in Washington and Paris, to bemoan the breakup of German consensus, particularly noting that the governing Christian Democrats (CDU) and their allies supported the deployment of Pershings and cruise missiles in Germany, while the Social Democrats (SPD) drifted into opposition to it after 1983. Yet well before 1989 a new middle ground was apparent, reflecting the primacy of German stakes in a stable Europe:

- Trade and humanitarian contacts across the East-West divide in Europe are a good thing in any season. Economic sanctions, for any purpose, are correspondingly bad.

- Arms control is similarly good, almost irrespective of agreements. More is better.

- Given the minimal threat of Soviet adventure in Europe, nuclear deterrence is a fact and would remain so, with many fewer nuclear weapons based in Germany.

- Given the minimal threat, foreign troops are a noisy, expensive bother. They need not go home, but should behave less as occupiers.

- The Western alliance must recognize special German interests.

This German consensus is not all new, but it does reflect both the inheriting of the SPD's clothes by the CDU and the seeping into mainstream politics of the antinuclear allergy.

Over the longer term, Gorbachev is also pushing the German question forward, probably without meaning to. He is doing so, in general, by raising the prospect of unfreezing the status quo in Europe and, more specifically, again unwittingly, by undermining the legitimacy of the remaining Stalinists in eastern Europe and in the German Democratic Republic above all. Those conservative eastern Europeans now find themselves sandwiched between the blandishments of the West and the reformers in Moscow.

This delegitimization is not for today, despite the recent waves of East German immigrants westward. Now, the regime commands at least grudging acquiescence from most of its citizens;[4] it can point to the economy and ask of Poles or Hungarians: What has reform done for you? Moreover, it has managed to bring its relationship with the Federal Republic to that of equals.

Yet by the logic of events set in motion by Moscow, reform is the order of the day and opening the East-West border a means. What place is there in such a logic for a neo-Stalinist rump Germany, justified by ideology, the division of Germany, and Soviet troops? And, more to the point, what more logical course for that rump than some form of association with the rest of Germany?

Why should Gorbachev risk tinkering with the core of a European order that has, whatever the rhetoric, served everyone save a few German politicians on Sunday? By the 1970s his predecessors had settled on a German policy combining a tight hold on East Germany and a limited détente with the Federal Republic. They pursued the course of seeking to loosen the Federal Republic's ties to the West without having to come near the question of whether they would like actually to succeed at that task.

Gorbachev might be driven to contemplate unprecedented risks, much as the imperative of reform at home now drives him to destabilize eastern Europe. In the past, foreign policy shifts have ensued from Soviet domestic politics: witness Soviet acceptance of Romania's limited independence and of the Austrian State Treaty, both of which owed something to intraparty maneuvering in the wake of Stalin's death. Or he might not have much choice. Events might reconfigure Moscow's German problem: who would have thought two decades ago that pan-German sentiments would be more alive in the East than the West, complete with a bizarre celebration of Luther's birthday?

As a thought-experiment, imagine a new Yalta, this time with the Europeans present. Could the United States and the western Europeans agree? If so, what would they ask of Moscow? And what would they be prepared to give in return? Would they want to withdraw all American troops from western Europe if Moscow took its from eastern Europe? Would Moscow ask? And what would any of the parties say about Germany? Would the Federal Republic settle for loose confederation with its eastern rump? Put differently, reflecting on the surprises but also the surprising continuity of the last 40 years of the European-American alliance: what new perspective would last for another 40 years?

Notes

1. Richard E. Neustadt, *Alliance Politics* (New York: Columbia University Press, 1970), p. 149.
2. This is the theme of Anton De Porte's fine book, *Europe between the Superpowers: The Enduring Balance* (New Haven: Yale University Press, 1979).
3. For instance, in a 1987 Enmid poll, 81 percent supported reunification, though only 8 thought it was possible within a decade. *The Economist*, June 6, 1987.
4. See A. James McAdams, "The Origins of a New Inner-German Relationship," in Larrabee, ed., *The Two German States and European Security* (New York: Macmillan Press, 1989).

The Priority of Constructing Western Europe

Pierre Hassner

One of the most striking features of the European-American relationship since 1945 has been the constant anxiety about its future. Did the end of World War II lead us into a world in which the Atlantic Ocean had permanently lost its geopolitical significance and America was in Europe for good, or into a provisional situation in which the American presence was supposed to be a stopgap solution paving the way to the reconstruction of a Europe that should take care of its own prosperity and security? At no time in these 45 years have contradictory trends not been combined to make the answer ambiguous and uncertain.

Change Not Yet?

In the second half of the postwar period, I have repeatedly engaged in the exercise of weighing the recurrent strains, the resilient structures, and the subterranean evolutions of the relationship. My central perception has always been the contrast between the rigidity of the geostrategic system and the evolution of society. Would the inflexible system always contain the evolving society, or would it finally be eroded or overthrown by society's repeated assaults? My answer has tended to be: the latter, eventually, but not just yet. As long as the two major factors that brought the United States into Europe—the presence of Soviet military power in eastern Europe and the inability of western Europe to balance it—existed, mutual irritation and centrifugal tendencies were unlikely to undo the "frustrated but frozen" Atlantic relationship.[1] Kennan's disengagement plans of the 1950s; de Gaulle's vision of the 1960s of Europe from the Atlantic to the Urals, the "Europeanization of

Europe" ideas of the German left in the early 1980s—all these were indications of a plausible and desirable long-range trend, but all were misleading for the middle term. They underestimated the rigidity of the system and, in particular, that of its main pillar, the Soviet empire, a rigidity compounded by the presence of nuclear weapons and by their power to freeze political situations, however abnormal.

Could it be that, for better or for worse, these basic elements are themselves shaken by the winds of change? What seems clear, at least, is that the cliché with which I started my evaluation of the European system in 1967—"Every period is by definition a period of transition but some are more transitional than others"[2]—applies even more to the next 20 years than it did to the last. Already by the mid-1960s, the death of Stalin and the outcome of the Cuban missile crisis had signaled the decline of the direct Soviet military threat to the West, while, conversely, the advent of nuclear parity was signaling the limits of extended deterrence and American protection. America's engagement in Vietnam was creating doubts and resentment between the United States and Europe; the Chinese, French, and Romanian challenges were raising the specter of polycentrism, West and East, and challenging the bipolar division; and the Federal Republic of Germany was beginning to search its way out of the Adenauer orthodoxy. Already then, various competing schemes for an "alternative to partition" and a European security system or "peaceful order" were emerging, only to be brutally squashed by the invasion of Prague in 1968.

In the years since, most of these trends and countertrends have continued making their way. Social and political movements in eastern and western Europe have had their spectacular victories followed by no less abrupt declines, the United States has alternated between syndromes of withdrawal and of reassertion, western Europe has vacillated between "Europessimistic" stagnation and renewed faith in the Common Market. But to see only a series of stop-and-go cycles would be shortsighted. Rather, what seemed to happen was a sharpening of the contradiction between system and society. In their different ways, the gaps between the two superpowers and their European allies had widened, and the legitimacy of the existing order grown thinner and thinner.

Yet, on the other hand, no plausible alternative order had emerged because western Europe was as far as ever from being able to defend itself, while the task was as far as ever from being superfluous. As François Duchêne once put it, the Soviets cannot withdraw their troops from eastern Europe because of their police function, and as long as the Soviets are in eastern Europe, western Europe needs the United States as a counterweight.[3] However, this objective need was less and less felt by the public, in particular by the younger generation in Germany, which was more and more resentful of the occupied status of its country. And so the alliance seemed really threatened for the first time because its two central protagonists, the United States and the Federal Republic, were less and less on the same wavelength, a situation it could much less tolerate than any other division. Still, the alliance was kept solidly alive by the lack of any alternative, because of the resilience of the one safely predictable part of the international scene—the Soviet empire.

Nothing Quiet on the Eastern Front?

Almost all of a sudden, in the middle 1980s, the situation seemed to reverse itself. While western Europe and America now seem on a moderate and compatible course at least in their view of East-West relations, after the turmoil and the sharp divergences of the early 1980s, the evolution in Poland and Hungary and, even more surprisingly, in Gorbachev's Soviet Union has made the communist world much less stable and predictable than its Western counterpart. While the sources of its ferment come precisely, in great part, from the contrast between the dynamism of modern, Western capitalist society and the stagnation or decrepitude of the communist system, today it is the decline of the latter that provides the major source of unpredictability, not least in intra-Western relations themselves.

The prophecy Raymond Aron is supposed to have uttered in his last conversation with Hedley Bull seems to be coming true much more quickly than he thought: "It is my view that the most important and indeed most neglected question in contemporary international relations scholarship is: what will the West do, when and if the Soviets decline? How we answer that question will perhaps determine whether there will be war or peace in our time."[4]

Indeed, it might be said that what used to be the most predictable element of the international system has become the most unpredictable, yet it still provides us with the trend that allows the safest long-range prediction, the death of Marxism-Leninism. The exhaustion of its legitimacy and the avowal of defeat by the leading elites of the major communist states in the face of economic failure and social decay seem as irreversible as any ideological trend can be. What seems quite unpredictable, however, is what will succeed it. What seems only slightly less unlikely than the revival of Marxism-Leninism is a smooth transition of the communist states to liberal democracy and capitalism. Even if the current reforms are successful and spread to the whole communist world, this is likely to happen through a succession of crises, hence of unpredictable situations.

If the reforms do not succeed, then it becomes even more difficult to ascertain how, for instance, the basic contradiction between political Westernization and economic Third Worldization in eastern Europe will work itself out, or what a post-Gorbachev future might look like, for it is bound to be a return neither to simple Brezhnevite stagnation nor to outright Stalinist terror. Among disintegration (possibly including civil war) relatively moderate military or technocratic rule, and an expansionist or, on the contrary, a retreating and retrenching Russian nationalism, the range of possibilities is wide open. So, too, is the range of Western reactions and of possibilities for intra-Western divergences.

A continuation of détente and rapprochement would—at least in the short run—be much less divisive for the Western alliance, as far as policies toward the East are concerned, than was the "new cold war" during the second half of the Carter administration and the first Reagan one. Today, there is no fundamental difference between Europe and the United States in attitudes toward the communist states. Yet, inevitably, the fading away of the military dimension will encourage the development of special relationships, such as those between the two Germanies or the superpowers, ones that are bound to compete with those that bind the West. The problem of American withdrawal and that of German unity are likely to loom ever larger.

If, on the other hand, the world enters into either a period of renewed confrontation or one of revolutionary disorder within the Soviet sphere, it is likely that the divisions created in the West by the crises over Afghanistan and Poland will reemerge with a vengeance. Policy decisions would reopen debate between hawks and doves. Europeans, particularly the West Germans, would be more inclined to favor a benevolent attitude and to find in the new situation a new justification for détente, while the United States, whose commitment to the latter has always been more conditional and which is likely to remain less deeply involved with the East, would be more tempted to return to a new form of cold war.

Even this prediction, however, must be heavily qualified. In particular, if the hardening or revolutionary disorders in the East occur after a relatively prolonged period of detente, the possibility cannot be excluded that American and European attitudes might turn around: the United States may by then have sufficiently turned away from Europe, at least psychologically, to react to events in the East with relative indifference. Conversely, the greater involvement of western Europeans may result in greater concern, a concern not always entirely benevolent in nature. Particularly, again, in the Federal Republic, disappointment with the political fruits of détente and irritation with its social and economic consequences—particularly concerning the increase of immigration from the East—may, just conceivably, lead to a reversal of attitudes.

In truth, what makes prediction so difficult is that the impact of East-West relations on European ones depends on the interplay of at least three types of factors. The most obvious is the political and military state of the East-West relationship. But the two others are becoming more important, precisely as this one is becoming less salient. The first of these is the decline of cohesion induced by the feeling of a common Soviet threat and by the constraints of a common defense. Economics usually is supposed to be a positive and peaceful activity concerned with production and consumption, while military strategy is seen as a negative one concerned either with destruction or with its prevention or limitation. Paradoxically, though, in European-American relations—and, in a different way, in East-West ones as well—the military dimension has played a stabilizing role and the economic one may be much more divisive.

Within the "trans-Atlantic bargain," both sides have made economic sacrifices for the sake of common security in front of the communist threat—the United States through direct aid and by encouraging European integration, hence the rise of a potential rival; the Europeans by the American deficit, hence allowing the United States to dispense with the austerity that they had to undergo themselves. Economic issues that, left to themselves, would have led to bitter recriminations were never allowed to escalate lest they undermine public support for the alliance. However, in the new situation they may be allowed to take their course and produce a fallout that, in turn, may damage the psychological and financial bases of the security link even further.

The paradox is that a somewhat parallel phenomenon may occur in the relations of western European states with their eastern neighbors, producing even less-predictable consequences for their relations with the United States. The ideological and military confrontation froze the division of Europe in two camps. It thus brought the contacts between the societies on opposite sides of the Iron Curtain to a minimum, thereby inducing a maximum of psychological, cultural, and economic frustration. Yet by the same token, it had a stabilizing effect: societies were relatively invulnerable to each other. The diminution of ideological and military confrontation, on the other hand, by increasing contacts of all sorts, also creates greater mutual vulnerabilities. This is obvious for the regimes of the East: witness the end to their jamming of Western broadcasts. Yet the problems created for Western societies by the easing of the constraints on emigration from the East may be almost as serious. The shock created in the Federal Republic by the immigration of 200,000 ethnic Germans from the East, its effect on the successes of the far right in Berlin and Frankfurt elections in 1989, the efforts of the government to limit the entry of Poles and Yugoslavs: all these are the most spectacular western European examples.

They are part of a more general phenomenon to which the United States and its Asian allies are far from immune (witness the problem at the U.S.–Mexican border and the plight of the boat people): as communist regimes begin opening up while economic inequalities persist or even increase between them and the capitalist world, East-West relations come to resemble even more North-South ones. The problem of refugees and immigration—whether from the East or from the South— becomes one of the major problems of the time. Within the West it should lead to more cooperative action for balancing access to the West with help to the East and the South, but it may lead to more centrifugal tendencies if Americans and Europeans become absorbed in relations with their respective neighbors (central Americans and Asians in one case, eastern Europeans and Mediterraneans in the other) or if they carry their quarrels over burden sharing and protectionism from the field of troops and goods to that of migrants and refugees.

Perhaps the best analysis of the general situation is that of the Italian commentator Arrigo Levi. He points out that all the ideological challenges to the West have been defeated and that, in the East and in the South, most of humankind aspires to a Western-type political and economic order. But he goes on to remark that the West is frightened by its own victory, and for good reason: with few exceptions, the communist nations and the Third World countries are unlikely to succeed in their conversion to democracy and capitalism. This failure will multiply the aspirations of hundreds of millions from these less-favored nations to share the prosperity and freedom of Europe and the United States by emigrating there. And the developed West seems equally unable either to integrate them without jeopardizing its own political and economic stability or to help them enough so that they may live in peace and freedom within their own borders.[5]

Even more generally, the decline of East-West confrontation is increasing the awareness and the priority both of domestic and of global problems. But whether this will lead, between Europe and the United States, to more community or to more estrangement, to more cooperation or to more conflict, to more stability or to more danger depends on the character of domestic evolutions on both sides of the Atlantic and on the nature of the global challenges. Ultimately it depends on the depth of the revolution in international affairs, from the politics of power and primacy to those of world order, from military intervention to economic cooperation, from "high politics," to "low politics," from "old thinking" to "new thinking."

End of History or End of a Cycle?

If history is defined by the succession of wars and revolutions, by the rise and breakdown of empires and hegemonies, are we living through a phase in a recurrent cycle or the end of history? I am tempted to answer that we live at the intersection of three different cycles—the short-run cycle of cold war and détente; the medium-run cycle of introversion and extroversion, or of isolationism and internationalism in American foreign policy; and the long-run cycle of rise and decline in Europe's historic role.

The successive phases of cold war and détente have sometimes lasted no more than a few years. Some American scholars have suggested 20–25-year cycles of expansion and retreat for the United States. Many have pronounced the diagnosis of "Eurosclerosis" or of terminal fatigue for a European continent exhausted by two world wars and several colonial ones, and incapable of standing up any longer for its own security, let alone for recovering its past role of grandeur.

Each of these views has some plausibility. But neither can be taken too seriously as a guide for the future. First, the uncertainty concerning the Soviet empire extends to its role in a grand historical vision: only twelve years ago, the task of Western policy was said to be to manage the rise of the Soviet Union to a global role; today it is said to be to manage its decline. The two views can be reconciled through believing both that the communist regimes are breaking down and that the vital energies of the Russian people, which have been stifled culturally and economically for seventy years, have yet to be released on the world scene.

Second, while East-West relations will probably always experience ups and downs, the dominant trend does seem to go toward conciliation. The new cold war of the late 1970s and early 1980s never eradicated all the achievements of the old détente, at least in Europe, and whatever the unpredictabilities in the Soviet Union and elsewhere, the new phase is likely to leave an even more lasting mark.

Third, the classical alternations of American attitudes seem to have become both more short-lived and more partial. After the "post-Vietnam" syndrome, the Reagan reassertion, highly successful as it was at a symbolic and rhetorical level, stopped far short of the pre-Vietnam readiness to use force, to run risks, or to call for sacrifices; and it seems already to have all but died out. Conversely, European passivity cannot be relied upon as a permanent trend: the Falklands War and its great popularity in England showed that traditional attitudes cannot be discounted. Europe's future may bring either renewed energy and ambition through the progress of European unity or the contrary, newly conflictive parochial or nationalist moods as a reaction to the strains of economic crises and their social and cultural shocks.

Without being *too* speculative, all I can do at this stage is register one structural change that seems irreversible (short of a nuclear or ecological crisis that brings a collapse of civilization) and one tentative opinion, a hunch based on a combination of philosophical belief (or prejudice) and fragmentary evidence.

The certainty is that nuclear weapons will continue to exist and exert to some degree their double effect—potential destruction and actual restraint. A further certainty is that the globalization of international politics will go on, that no great state or society, including China and the Soviet Union, can any longer close itself for any length of time to the penetration of modern mass communication and, through it, the attraction of modern patterns of consumption. These patterns will continue to provoke neotraditionalist and xenophobic reactions, but ones that will, in the coming period, be incapable of keeping any important part of the developed world in a state of economic or spiritual autarky. Between Europe and America, while political and economic conflict may increase, and while strategic solidarity may decline, two myths must be discarded: that of an autarchic "Fortress Europe" and that of an isolationist America.

As to the general character of international politics, the trends connected with modernity will continue—the "disenchantment of the world," the decline of traditional communities, the progress of permissiveness and of compassion, the prevalence of individualism (both spiritual and economic) over collectivism, particularly in military efforts and sacrifices. What is in doubt is whether they represent a fundamental change in world history or the end of a Spenglerian cycle, with its familiar components—the role of money, the growth of big cities and the lawlessness associated with them, the proliferation of superstitions, and the frantic search for escapist distractions—all connected with the decline of great civilizations. If we are seeing the end of a cycle, it will be followed one day by new Caesars and new prophets, by a new age of heroism, austerity, and religion and, possibly, of conquest and fanaticism.

I am inclined to think we are headed in that direction over the long run. That inclination derives from a belief in the complexity of human nature and in the notion that fundamental features, like the search for absolutes and the need for community and for enemies, can be repressed for whole periods but not eradicated forever. It is strengthened by certain phenomena, like the apparent increase in individual violence accompanying the decline of war and revolution. But, fortunately, the current trend is unlikely to be reversed for the next 20 years, which is the focus of this essay. At least that is true for the West; even though the Soviet Union is today the most vocal proponent of world order politics, both the East and the South are more likely than the West to experience and propagate a partial return to disorder in the coming years.

Three Possible Outcomes

Rather than any further attempt at prediction, I suggest three possible scenarios for the next 20 years, which represent three combinations of permanent structures with the process of the trends and countertrends I have mentioned. The first, and for the time being the most likely, depicts a move from the two alliances to a security system based on cooperation between the two superpowers, the two halves of Europe, and the two Germanies. Western Europe and the United States would drift apart militarily and politically while remaining closely linked economically and culturally.

The second, and most dangerous, would be a turn from benign to violent fragmentation and a reappearance of some of the features of the 1930s—nationalism; domestic crises, accompanied by a search for scapegoats; a renewal of the Soviet threat with the odds for a united Western response even less favorable than today.

The third, which would be the most desirable and, not unexpectedly, is the least likely, would involve an orderly devolution of power from the United States to Europe. It would combine a parallel opening to the East, leading to an end of the cold war and the division of Europe, with a sense of Western solidarity and a common global responsibility.

The first is the only one I shall consider in any detail, since it requires less in the way of gazing into a crystal ball and more analysis of present trends.

Negatively, these trends represent a movement away from the reality of bipolarity and the ideal of an Atlantic Community, but also from a Fortress Europe and the ideal of a Third Force. They correspond to the logic of cooperation prevailing over that of the arms race, the logic of détente prevailing over that of cold war, the logic of interdependence prevailing over that of protectionism, the logic of an expanding European Community prevailing over that of a tightening one. The question remains, however, whether this trend toward the declining salience of Atlantic ties within the context of a wider East-West reconciliation and toward an opening of the European Community to new competition from America and Asia and to new membership (particularly from east central Europe and the Mediterranean) will lead to greater unity or greater fragmentation.

In security terms, the spectacular decline in the perception of the Soviet threat will continue, along with the popular allergy to nuclear weapons, particularly land-based ones owned by foreigners. These two phenomena, combined with economic constraints, will lead to a considerable reduction in military budgets, in nuclear weapons, and in stationed foreign troops. How far will these trends go? General disarmament can be excluded, and, I would argue, so can the total elimination of nuclear weapons. On the other hand, the total withdrawal of superpower troops and nuclear weapons from continental Europe cannot be excluded, but it does not seem likely, if only for reasons of political stability in Europe and of nuclear proliferation elsewhere. Rather, the trend seems toward "minimum deterrence," entailing certainly the preservation of some second-strike, sea-based capacity by the existing nuclear powers and perhaps also a symbolic nuclear presence in central Europe.

On the conventional side, serious progress toward a restructuring of military postures in the direction of "defensive defense" or of a "structural inability to attack" cannot be ruled out. This would certainly doom attempts by the North Atlantic Treaty Organization (NATO) to move to a strategy based on counterattack or mobility, and it probably would, when combined with the demise or decline of theater nuclear weapons, pose serious threats to the existing strategy of flexible response. At the same time, much greater changes would be imposed on Soviet strategy, which would have to alter the whole character of its posture, based on surprise and preemption. But this too cannot be excluded.

Both sides, then, would find it very hard to implement central tenets of their strategies, deliberate escalation in one case, a combined arms offensive in the other. Operational options would be sacrificed in favor of political considerations. These would be concerned with reassuring both the other side and allied populations, rather than integrating the respective alliances, since defensive postures would probably be more territorial and hence more national.

If the Conventional Forces in Europe (CFE) talks succeed (and, even by the standards of the Mutual and Balanced Force Reduction (MBFR) negotiations, 20 years should not be a inaccessible deadline), they will have established a rough parity or balance of conventional forces. But this would not mean a real balance of power, for the Soviet Union, by virtue of its size and location, would maintain what might be called a residual, potential, or existential superiority. This would be balanced, if at all, by a residual, potential, or existential American or western European deterrent. In any case, the nature of the European security system would change.

From the beginning of the cold war, the system was founded on the equilibrium of the two alliances, led by the two superpowers and based on the physical presence in Europe of their troops and, after the 1950s, of their nuclear weapons. The structural fault lines of the Atlantic alliance—its geographical discontinuity and political polycentrism—were compensated, once American superiority was gone, by interpenetration: in particular the presence of U.S. and other allied troops and nuclear weapons in the Federal Republic was supposed to blur the difference between Americans and Europeans, and between nuclear and non-nuclear members of NATO.

With the prevalence of cooperation and negotiation over confrontation and deterrence, and of conventional over nuclear forces, the existing vertical security system would break up into two parallel, horizontal "security partnerships." The first would be the superpower one, based on a strategic dialogue between the United States and the Soviet Union that surely would extend to permanent efforts to concert over regional security issues, including those in Europe, and that might include partial protection of their respective territories through antimissile defense. The second would be the continental one, based on the negotiated restructuring of conventional forces.

The superpowers would still be present, but the central role would be that of the European middle powers themselves, especially that of the two German states.

On both levels, the respective partners would probably find more security and certainly more freedom of action. What would suffer is the links between the two systems—that is, the two alliance organizations, NATO's strategy of escalation, and the British and the French independent nuclear forces, which would find themselves more or less hanging in the air. The loss would be greater on the Western side, if only because the Soviet Union would be more present in both systems than the United States. That would be so for reasons of geography: Eastern military continuity exists naturally, but the Western one has to be artificially created and maintained.

Perhaps, however, these military misgivings would either become irrelevant or be compensated for by political and economic developments. Clearly, European security is less about war than about peace, less about avoiding nuclear or conventional confrontations, let alone affecting their outcome, than about redrawing the political map of Europe. In this sense, the meaning of the CFE talks may indeed be, as both the American and Soviet foreign ministers indicated in their opening speeches in March 1989, the attempt to overcome the division of Europe. The logic of the model outlined here involves the creation, de facto at least, of a central European zone, with some, perhaps all, eastern European states acquiring a quasi-neutral status or, at any rate, getting more detached from the Soviet Union and closer to the West, and the ties between the two German states being developed into some kind of reassociation.

Unquestionably, the gravitational pull in this evolution is toward the West as far as political regimes or cultural influences are concerned. But just as unmistakably, this evolution would involve a certain reorientation of Berlin, of the Federal Republic, and of European integration away from an Atlantic and toward a pan-European direction, from NATO toward the "common European house" popularized by Gorbachev. In particular, Germany would play a much more active role in the East, while the United States and Canada would still be present in Europe but in a more marginal way.

Politics and Economics

What would be the institutional and economic consequences for the European Community and its external relations? It seems clear that the model involves what in European Community jargon is called *élargissement* (enlargement) at the expense of *approfondissement* (deepening). In line with the preferences of the Federal Republic, the European Community would be enlarged to include first Austria, then Hungary, then the other eastern European states (perhaps at first through associate status), as well as Turkey. Much of the Community's energy in the coming two decades would be aimed at bridging the gap between the two halves of Europe. What is not so clear is what this would entail for the economic relations of the Community with the rest of the world, particularly with the United States.

One view is that, economically and technologically, these developments will increase both the gap and the frictions between the European Community and the United States. In the view of a Soviet specialist quoted by Angela Stent: "By the year 2000 there will be two economic axes: US-Japan, the high-tech, microelectronic axis, and Western Europe and Eastern Europe, the low-tech, traditional, complementary axis."[6] Wolfgang Berner and William Griffith think that "the issue of West German technology and transfer credits to the Soviet Union and the Communist countries of Central and Eastern Europe is likely to remain a recurrent problem for Bonn in its relationship with Washington. In this respect, at least, protectionism and West German policy toward Communist Central and Eastern Europe are organically connected."[7]

I wonder, however, whether an enlarged Community focused on its pan-European ties would be a protectionist one. It seems more likely that it would lack the cohesion or the political will to pursue any coherent common policy at all. External relations would be decided above all by the member states themselves, particularly by the Federal Republic which has no inter-est in being imprisoned in a low-technology ghetto and no intention of doing so. Rather, competitive interdependence with the United States and Japan is likely to continue and, in the absence of a strong Community, to be dominated by these two. The Federal Republic would continue being active both in the world economic league, with the United States and Japan, and in the all-European league, with the Soviet Union and eastern Europe. It would, however, have less chance of economic and technological success in the first and of political success in the second than if a common western European policy could be made to function.

Raymond Aron used to say that the sign that a region is included in the cold war is that power relations are turned upside down—with superpowers needing their smaller allies and being blackmailed by them. With the waning of the cold war, real power relations may be reasserting themselves. And this would mean a Europe dominated militarily (or at least geo-politically) by the Soviet Union, economically and culturally (or at least in technology and mass culture) by the United States and Japan, and internally (certainly at the economic level, prob-ably at the political and perhaps even at the military one) by West Germany. This is a price that the other Europeans, West and East, could find disagreeable to their national or collective pride but well worth paying if it brings them a better chance of peace, prosperity, and freedom. And so, indeed, it may.

The weakness of the model, however, is that it assumes a relatively bland, harmonious evolution without a major domes-tic or international crisis. Yet, if my analysis in the first part of this chapter has any validity, this is not the most likely course of events. Suppose the Soviet empire refuses to fade away grace-fully. Suppose that, rather than imploding, it explodes or gath-ers its last energies for a new attempt at escaping its difficulties through military reassertion. Suppose a half- or wholly eman-cipated eastern Europe falls prey to its old nationalist antago-nisms, or the failure of economic reform brings forth, in Poland and in Hungary, strong nationalist leaders of Milosevic's type, and Yugoslavia itself slides into civil war. Suppose the opening of borders between the two Europes and the two Germanies triggers the xenophobic reactions of which recent West German elections have given foretaste. Suppose the triumphant capitalism of the 1980s is shaken by a more serious crash than that of 1987. The world would then have most of the ingredients of the interwar period, complete with the collapse of empires, the struggle between rival nationalisms, and the domestic and social crises leading to the search for scapegoats. A fragmented Atlantic alliance and a diluted European Community would be powerless to forestall, to manage, or to contain these developments.

This is why, much as I value both trans-Atlantic and pan-European cooperation, both the sharing of global responsibilities and the overcoming of Europe's division, I would still cast my vote for a priority on western Europe. Only if the European Community succeeds in gaining some economic, political, and military autonomy can it play a coherent and constructive role on either the world or the all-European scene. To be sure, a provisional priority on western Europe would lead to accusations of constructing a Fortress Europe, of acting against the spirit of free trade or against that of "new thinking." But in the long run any genuine cooperation must be based on balance, and only a western European power can be both a valid interlocutor for a powerful United States and Soviet Union, and an effective stabilizer if either or both enter a vagarious period.

Between globalism and nationalism, between capitalist interdependence and a Soviet-inspired "common European house," an autonomous western Europe starts as a poor third. But it has a fighting chance, even without accepting the exaggerations that surround the myth of 1992. And given the stakes, if it has a chance, it is worth a try.

Notes

1. See my "Frustrated but Frozen: Europe and the Atlantic Relationship," *International Journal* (Spring 1984).
2. See my *Change and Security in Europe*, Adelphi Papers No. 45 and 48, (London: Institute for International Strategic Studies, 1968).

3. François Duchêne, "A New European Defense Community," *Foreign Affairs* (October 1971).
4. Quoted by Kurt M. Campbell, "Prospects and Consequences of Soviet Decline," in Joseph Nye, Graham T. Allison, and Albert Carnesale, eds., *Fateful Visions: Avoiding Nuclear Catastrophe* (Cambridge, MA: Ballinger, 1988), p. 153.
5. See his "L'autumo delle sommoss Faloscono le ideology alternative all'Occidente," *Corriere della Sera*, October 15, 1988.
6. "Technology Transfer to Eastern Europe: Paradoxes, Policies, Prospects," in William E. Griffith, ed., *Central and Eastern Europe: The Opening Curtain?* (Boulder, CO: Westview Press, 1989), p. 100.
7. Wolfgang Berner and William E. Griffith, "West German Policy towards Central and Eastern Europe," in Griffith, ed., p. 351.

Rebalancing the
U.S.–European–Soviet Triangle

David P. Calleo

The future of the triangular relationship of the United States, Europe, and the Soviet Union seems more unpredictable in this coming decade than it has been at any time since the beginning of the postwar era. Present trends raise the prospect of a major recasting of Europe's postwar order. Both superpowers could retreat from their confrontation across the middle of Germany. Eastern European states could be genuinely "finlandized"— even if they remained militarily neutral or under Soviet influence, they would have a far wider margin for diversity in their national arrangements and would be more open economically, politically, and culturally. The Soviet Union, no longer pressing its bid for European hegemony, might also be more open to collaborative relations with the West, particularly in Europe. The United States could give up its hegemonic role as the principal manager of Western European security. A western European coalition, allied to the United States, could become the principal political and military counterbalance to a less-threatening Soviet presence in Europe. That coalition might also become the principal economic partner for a Soviet Union bent on at least partial Westernization of its political economy.

Opportunities and Risks

In effect, these changes would amount to the transition from the bipolar Europe of superpower confrontation to a more plural or "European" Europe, where the two superpowers are no longer the central dominators of the system but become more peripheral participants. A European evolution along these lines is no longer fanciful. In general, the Soviet Union is clearly showing signs of serious overstrain from its traditional geopolitical ambitions. So, I would argue, is the United States, with its large fiscal and external deficits, and rapidly growing foreign debt. For both superpowers, Europe is likely to seem an ideal place to cut back.

The Soviet occupation of eastern Europe seems more and more a liability. The huge military deployments provide doubtful benefits to Soviet security, since they originally provoked and have continued to sustain a massive Western rearmament. The states in the Soviet sphere have traditionally considered themselves central European, or even Western, in their cultural and economic orientation. After 40 years they still do not willingly or naturally fit within a Russian empire. In the West, the American military protectorate seems increasingly anomalous and unsustainable, even if everyone would prefer it to continue. Western Europe contains several of the world's historic great powers, major economic and military states in their own right, closely linked in an increasingly effective economic union. In short, although the bipolar European system has lasted and kept the peace for nearly half a century, there is reason to believe its days are numbered.

Such a prospect causes understandable apprehension. A plural, or European, Europe will not automatically be peaceful. It certainly was not so in the past. Europe remains the only contested part of the world where the stakes make nuclear war a clear possibility. And there are larger implications for global order. American global predominance has been closely linked to the Atlantic alliance, which has agglomerated a great preponderance of strategic, political, economic, and cultural power for the West. A more plural Europe, with western Europe more self-sufficient, means a more plural world in general.

Geopolitical analysts argue that plural systems are by their very nature less stable and peaceful than hegemonic ones. An economic corollary holds that plural systems are inherently protectionist. Liberal world economic systems are sustainable, it is said, only under the patronage of a benevolent hegemonic power, predominant enough to maintain the rules and pay a disproportionate share of the system's general costs. A general tendency toward protectionism has been clearly observable as American economic primacy has slipped in recent decades.

The evolution to a more plural Europe also raises the fear of a radical geopolitical shift that would link all or part of western Europe and the Soviet Union. This link could take the Soviet-dominated form long feared as western Europe's or Germany's finlandization. A pan-European alliance could also be more balanced or even European-dominated. But analysts accustomed to regarding U.S.–Soviet relations as a zero-sum game see any close Soviet-European relationship as a mortal threat to American interests.

Yet I believe the broad adjustments are most likely to render such a Europe stable and benign. These adjustments mean "rebalancing the triangle" of American, European, and Soviet roles: the superpowers should withdraw from their military confrontation in Europe and give vigorous attention to putting their own domestic affairs in order. A more cohesive, assertive, and self-reliant western European coalition is the necessary counterpart.

This rebalancing is essential not only for stabilizing a changing European order but also for sustaining a healthy equilibrium in the world's political economy as a whole. Western rebalancing is essential for the strategic and political health of the Atlantic alliance, regardless of what Gorbachev achieves in the Soviet sphere. By prescribing a rebalancing of the American position along with the Soviet, I do not mean to suggest that America's role in Europe has been like that of the Soviet Union or that America's own national problems are similar. Indeed, the changes that now make that world more plural—the recovery of Europe and Japan, and the rise of independent political and economic powers in the Third World—reflect the great success of America's postwar strategy.

But if the postwar liberal economy is to survive the transition to a more plural geopolitical order, the United States must itself adjust to the changed situation; it must, in other words, come to terms with the success of its own policy. In particular, it must be careful not to fall into perennial and structured economic disequilibrium with the rest of the world. Otherwise, it risks becoming a "hegemon in decay," an overstretched power that tries to support its position by exploiting the remnants of its hegemony. The most predictable outcome is that it undermines itself and breaks up the global system into competing protectionist blocs.

Part of the U.S. adjustment must be directly geopolitical. One of the critical elements in America's fiscal disarray is a military budget that the national political economy is no longer willing to sustain. The most obvious remedy is a policy of "devolution" within the North Atlantic Treaty Orgainzation (NATO). The savings could be substantial and the move is called for, in any event, for sound strategic and political reasons. But the United States cannot succeed alone. "Devolution" requires a corresponding repartition of responsibilities with America's principal allies, above all with the western Europeans.

All these arguments are simply a way of noting what should be obvious: the triangular rebalancing of Europe and the general readjustment of the global system to a more plural order are closely interdependent. A more cohesive and assertive western Europe has become a sine qua non for both. I take up these topics in turn.

Comforts of the Status Quo

The reasons for the persistence of the postwar status quo in Europe are well known. Both superpowers have had good reasons to preserve it. For the United States, NATO has contained the Soviet Union on its own home ground. In partnership with western Europe, the United States became the world's dominant power, able to promote a liberal world political economy that bears a fair resemblance to its historic dreams. For the Soviet Union, its eastern European empire has seemed the major recompense for the terrible sufferings of World War II, as well as the principal guarantee against any recurrence. And eastern Europe has provided the Soviets with an international sphere of their own, which has nourished their pretensions to rival America as a global superpower.

The reasons for Europe's acquiescence vary. The eastern European states have had little choice. For western European states, the Soviet threat has made an American military protectorate welcome. Bipolar partition has also kept the "German problem" comfortably submerged. The smaller powers instinctively prefer a distant to a local hegemon. The major powers have also made themselves comfortable. Meanwhile, they have made the European Community (EC) an effective means for advancing their economic interests.

French and British policies have had a certain fundamental similarity. Both countries, once preeminent global powers, have strategic nuclear forces, large navies, and limited involvement in continental European defense. Rhetoric aside, perhaps the most significant difference is that Britain has generally distrusted any distinctive European cooperation, whereas France has promoted a European economic and political coalition. But while this European coalition has also had certain obvious military implications, the French have always drawn back from pursuing them wholeheartedly.

Although French policy has maintained a high degree of continuity in its rhetoric, and perhaps in its fundamentals, it has adjusted to changing circumstances. Gaullist France denounced Europe's bipolar division, launched its own détente policy, attacked the American role in Vietnam, complained about the dollar's international position, and finally withdrew from NATO's integrated military arrangements. As the Soviets moved toward strategic parity in the 1970s, the French grew more cordial toward NATO and began to develop close bilateral military cooperation with the West Germans. Nevertheless, French leaders repeatedly disclaimed any intention of rejoining NATO and President Mitterrand went out of his way to declare that France would not, in the foreseeable future, "Europeanize" its nuclear deterrent. France's European military commitment has remained very much "on the cheap."

Postwar West Germany's reconciliation to the status quo is the most surprising. West German policy has juggled three vital interests: Atlantic, European, and national—the last defined by West Germany's own postwar division. It has developed each option as fully as has seemed possible without endangering the others. The Federal Republic's first chancellor, Konrad Adenauer, gave firm and organic Western ties priority over national reunification. West Germany became America's principal partner in Europe's defense. Meanwhile, the Social Democratic opposition and some elements of Adenauer's own Christian Democrats continued to argue that only a neutral Germany, floating between East and West, could achieve reunification, and might even be able to reconstitute a German-led *Mitteleuropa* as a buffer between the superpowers. Adenauer was skeptical that reunification could be reconciled with democracy and prosperity, and doubted that the superpowers would permit reunification in any event.

Adenauer's European course led to a parallel special relationship with France. The European Coal and Steel Community, the European Economic Community (EEC) and Euratom followed. By the early 1960s, the Franco-German special relationship had begun to make itself felt in Atlantic diplomacy. France and West Germany had found common cause in resisting British efforts to dilute the EEC into a free-trade area. They soon found themselves opposed to Kennedy's efforts to consolidate a superpower détente in Europe, which de Gaulle called a "new Yalta" at Europe's expense. Instead, he proposed his "Europe from the Atlantic to the Urals"—a formula that suggested a balanced pan-European system to replace the superpower division imposed by World War II. Within such a system, de Gaulle argued, Germany could find an acceptable form of national reunification and the countries of eastern Europe could find their liberty. The German problem could be solved by the Europeans themselves.

As American and French détente advanced, the West Germans were ready for an eastern policy of their own. In effect, German *Ostpolitik* became a strategy to transform the status quo by accepting it. West German relations with the Soviets improved and the way was opened for increasingly intimate relations with the German Democratic Republic (GDR). Once the cold war barriers were down, the Germans were counting on their economic weight to exert a powerful attraction.

To the French, and indeed the Americans, this began to look more like *Mitteleuropa* than *Pan-Europa*. But by the mid-1970s, the limitations of a national German *Ostpolitik* had grown apparent. The Federal Republic's west European and Atlantic ties had grown too deeply rooted for an adventurous Eastern policy. And the Soviets under Brezhnev could not develop a political economy fit for intimate trade and investment relations with western Europe. The Soviets continued a relentless military buildup, in itself a cause and a compensation for their economic stagnation.

By the mid-1970s, the Federal Republic's policy had become essentially defensive—to guard its comfortable berth within the postwar dispensation. Like Britain and France, it had made the best of its situation in the postwar order. Any real change in national policy could be expected only in response to broader changes in the postwar international order. Real change in Europe would come only if the global system beyond Europe began to alter.

The NATO Problem

Since NATO has always been in essence an American nuclear protectorate, its effectiveness was naturally called into question as the Soviets achieved strategic parity in the mid-1970s, a point that need not be rehearsed here. Europeans and Americans have anyway long differed on NATO's strategy. The United States insisted that NATO adopt "flexible response"—a strategy that contemplates a long series of limited but escalating reactions, from conventional to nuclear warfare, designed to stop any Soviet thrust into Europe at the lowest level possible. Europeans, by contrast, traditionally have believed their greatest security comes from the probability that any major Soviet attack in Europe will elicit a nuclear response that will soon engulf the national territories of the superpowers themselves. No one, they believe, would deliberately initiate an all-out intercontinental nuclear war. But there is a danger, they imagine, of a European war rationalized by the presumption that it can be kept limited. They suspect that America's flexible response strategy encourages just such a presumption.

This fundamental strategic tension between America and its European allies, while ultimately irreconcilable, was nevertheless managed relatively easily throughout NATO's first 30 years. The various compromises—flexible response, British and French deterrents, U.S. nuclear forces in NATO, or participation in NATO's Nuclear Planning Group—seemed adequate so long as the strategic balance was heavily weighted in favor of the Americans.

By the mid-1970s, however, the tension was not so easily managed. In the 1970s, it was widely argued, the U.S. position was becoming less than parity. A Soviet first strike could destroy most of America's land-based aircraft and missiles. The United States, its arsenal limited to the then less-accurate sea-based missiles, could only respond by a counter-city attack, which would invite a similar massive Soviet attack on American cities. Under such circumstances, any American president would forego retaliation and accept Soviet terms, it was argued, rather than escalate to the virtual annihilation of both sides.

The Carter administration suggested closing this window of vulnerability with a new generation of mobile land-based missiles. The Reagan administration advanced its celebrated Strategic Defense Initiative. Neither solution won sufficient public credibility or support.

Not surprisingly, the American strategic debate was paralleled by a major crisis over nuclear deterrence within NATO— that over intermediate-range nuclear forces (INF). While western Europeans responded to the general situation by increasing their own military forces and intensifying their cooperation with each other,[1] the decisive struggle was in the Federal Republic. Christian Democratic Chancellor Helmut Kohl took up the cause. The victory of his coalition in 1983 appeared, among other things, a resounding assertion of Adenauer's old priority of security over reunification. When deployment of U.S. missiles began late in the year, NATO seemed to have managed a firm reaffirmation of its traditional arrangements, contrary strategic trends notwithstanding.

The triumph was short-lived. At the Reykjavik summit in 1986, President Reagan and the new Soviet leader, Mikhail Gorbachev, both accepted the "zero option." The Reagan administration claimed a major victory. Privately, European governments were shocked and deeply disappointed. Their real fear was not the Soviet SS-20 missiles, per se, but a decoupling of European defense from the American nuclear deterrent. Reagan's rhetoric compounded their dismay. At Reykjavik, he joined Gorbachev in hoping for a "denuclearization" of Europe. In his enthusiasm for the Strategic Defense Initiative, he repeatedly proffered the vision of the whole world free from nuclear weapons.

Whatever the president intended, it was natural for Europeans to infer that such rhetoric, and the INF agreement itself, was the logical American reaction to the altered nuclear balance. Reagan's conservatives had arrived in power denouncing the Strategic Arms Limitations agreements (SALT) for accepting strategic parity. By 1984, they had come up with no alternative, except an implausible total strategic defense. As America's elites and public began to comprehend the altered risks of extending nuclear deterrence to Europe, a tendency toward disengagement seemed natural. Hence, the Reagan administration was itself pressing for arms control agreements—particularly those that would phase out or limit America's nuclear commitment to Europe.

These trends point toward an obvious conclusion: America cannot continue to guarantee Europe's security. For Europe's major powers the long postwar vacation from their own responsibility for European security is coming to an end. In a multipolar world, where the United States no longer has strategic superiority and nuclear deterrence is no longer a superpower monopoly, if there is to be a military balance in Europe, the Europeans will have to take the primary responsibility for it.

This is not to say that the Atlantic alliance is doomed. If America can no longer be a hegemonic protector, it can certainly remain an ally. With or without American hegemony, the geopolitical rationale for a trans-Atlantic alliance endures. For Europe, America's strategic aid in balancing the Soviets is likely to remain essential. For America, a European alliance is the most efficient and rewarding way to contain Soviet power in Eurasia. In theory, both interests could be best served by the creation of a more self-sufficient European "pillar" within a transformed NATO.

Economic Parallels

This pluralist military logic seems all the more forceful because it runs parallel to broad trends in the world economy. America's economic predominance has diminished significantly since the 1950s. The rapid growth of Japan, various Third World countries, and Europe itself has produced a more balanced global economic order. This pluralist trend was reinforced by the success of OPEC and the consolidation of the European Community.

America's relative decline was a predictable consequence of its own postwar policy, and indeed a striking mark of that policy's success. The United States had set out to promote the recovery of the European and Japanese economies, along with development in the Third World. Such a policy implied a relative shrinking of the historically unnatural American predominance that existed after World War II. A liberal global economy could not be stabilized, it was thought, without a more even distribution of economic strength.

Forty years later, the fruits of America's policy had grown apparent. World capitalism had blossomed under a veritable *Pax Americana*. At the same time, the U.S. economic condition was posing severe problems of adjustment for both the United States and its major allies. For the United States the problem had become how to keep its relative decline from becoming a real degeneration of national economic vitality. For the world in general, the problem had become how to manage a system so dependent on the benevolent hegemony of its leading power, after that power had grown weaker and less benevolent. By the end of the 1980s, the prolonged failure of America and its allies to cope with this dual problem was having increasingly serious consequences, as the reinforcing and compounding American disequilibria pressed ever more heavily on the global economy.

The American economy itself had settled into some very bad habits. Starting in the mid-1970s, it gradually developed a large structural fiscal deficit at home and large and intractable trade and current account deficits abroad. By the 1980s, these deficits had reached previously inconceivable proportions. With the American economy's exceptionally high rate of consumption and low rate of saving, the deficits could not be financed out of national resources. By the mid-1980s, the United States had passed from being the world's major creditor to its major debtor.

From 1977 to 1987, the net federal debt jumped from 23 percent to nearly 38 percent of gross national product, a level roughly twice that of the Federal Republic of Germany and three times that of Japan or France.[2] The huge indebtedness took place in a period when there was no war, and when American gross fixed capital formation and real fixed investment tended to lag behind that of Japan, Germany, or France.[3]

Broadly speaking, over the postwar decades the United States has gradually settled into a pattern of following two alternating macroeconomic formulas. In one formula, a large fiscal deficit is financed with easy money—which means a boom, rising inflation, a falling dollar, and an improving trade balance. In the other, a large fiscal deficit is combined with tight money—which means high interest rates, a recession, a heavy inflow of foreign capital, a high dollar, a deteriorating trade balance, and a "debt crisis." Both formulas answer the ever-urgent need to finance the excess of spending over resources. In one, the government prints money; in the other, it borrows back from foreigners the money it printed earlier. Each formula eventually produces distinctive bad effects. When these accumulate sufficiently, policymakers turn from one policy to the other.

In one way or another, this alternation has been going on since the late 1960s. Politicians and many analysts have come to look at it with some complacency. It does represent a certain rough systemic justice. As the global hegemon providing security for its rich allies, the United States carries exceptional military burdens, which contribute significantly to the unmanageable fiscal situation. Manipulating monetary policy, and hence the dollar, to finance these deficits passes on to America's rich allies some of the security costs that they refuse to assume directly.

However, complacent analysis seems increasingly inappropriate. It discounts the possibility of a financial collapse as the monetary balancing act grows more and more precarious. It overlooks the long-term consequences for America of its rapidly rising indebtedness. Moreover, America's profligacy prevails during what is anyway a delicate period for world free trade. Since the 1970s, the world economy has faced difficult problems of adjustment. A broad revolution in the development, production, and marketing of manufactures has put all advanced economies in acute competition with one another to master the latest technology. At the same time, the spread of industrialization to Third World countries with cheap labor threatens the high standard of living and broad welfare capitalism of these same advanced countries—a threat also to the foundations of their domestic political systems.

A powerful trend toward mercantilism and protectionism could be expected under any circumstances. But in an environment where monetary stability has broken down, thanks to the indiscipline of the leading capitalist economy, the trend is greatly reinforced. Where no firm rules regulate the monetary systems, governments can hardly be expected to refrain from intervening to secure a favorable exchange rate or competitive environment generally. As markets grow more and more disorderly, countries can be expected to give up on a liberal global system and to try, instead, to create orderly conditions within a more limited sphere. Protectionism is the natural reaction, and a world of blocs seems the most practical option. These were the general tendencies that came to the fore as the prewar liberal economy broke down in the financial disorders of the late 1920s.

America's strategic and economic difficulties are in many ways reinforcing. So long as the United States tries to maintain its hegemonic military protectorate over western Europe, the diminished U.S. strategic position implies logically a greater emphasis on conventional deterrence or short-range nuclear forces. A NATO strategy that relies on short-range nuclear weapons seems increasingly unacceptable to the Federal Republic. Given the high cost of providing U.S. ground forces for Europe, America's pressing fiscal difficulties and squeeze on the military budget, a serious U.S. effort to upgrade NATO's conventional posture would clash head-on with any serious effort to bring U.S. macroeconomic policy under control. Thus, strategic trends and fiscal difficulties combine to put the American hegemonic position in NATO under increasing strain. From this broad geopolitical perspective, that role seems self-defeating.

European Adjustments

While American policy has been resisting the obvious, Europeans have been making their own adjustments. In reaction to the increasingly chaotic international economic environment, the European Community has grown progressively more integrated. After a failure earlier in the decade, 1979 saw the establishment of a new European Monetary System (EMS), promoted by a joint Franco-German initiative, in part a reaction to the simmering West German–American quarrel over monetary policy during the Carter administration. The Common Market has also reached out, to encompass Greece, Spain, and Portugal. More intimate accommodations with Austria and Turkey appear likely, as do more extensive agreements with the Soviet bloc's Council for Mutual Economic Assistance (COMECON). Altogether, the European Community now forms the world's largest and richest market. At least as liberal commercially as its American and Japanese rivals, it is also well positioned for a more autarkic path should the global trading system start to break down.

The continuing economic tribulations of the 1980s have provided renewed incentives for further European cooperation. Hence the Single European Act of 1987, with its broad agenda of integrating measures scheduled to be completed by 1992. These measures have caught the public's imagination and led to a rebirth of federalist rhetoric and expectations. The expectations will almost certainly be disappointed, while the rhetoric hides the EC's true character.

This point deserves some discussion, since it seems so significant for understanding Europe's future configuration. The reality of Europe's political and economic integration has long since outgrown the old-fashioned federalist formulas. As initially imagined by Jean Monnet and his followers in Europe and America, economic integration was to rob Europe's traditional nation-states of their effectiveness and legitimacy, which would be transferred to the new Community structures. Europe's success was linked to the emergence of a new federal state. In reality, however, the EC has not eliminated the traditional states but rejuvenated them. Working within the Community structure, Europe's states exercise substantially more control over their respective national economic environments than they otherwise would. Their loss of sovereignty within that structure is largely abstract, their gain is eminently concrete. As a result, the states have not faded away. Their persistence leads to the view that their cooperation has failed—a perception that seems more and more anomalous as their collaboration intensifies.

Part of the problem stems from an excessive abstract notion of sovereignty. In the legalistic formulations of lawyers and political scientists, "sovereign" states exercise absolute control over their territories and economies. But historically, modern European states have generally been highly open to each other and, therefore, highly interdependent. Does that mean they have never been sovereign? Perhaps a more useful definition of sovereignty would focus more on the idea of self-determination. For a state, this means not only freedom from external domination, but also a capacity for delivering what its society wants. Today, the sovereign isolation envisioned in the legalistic formulas could only come by sacrificing a large part of the economic welfare and human values that have been the primary goals of Europe's states since World War II. The European states' cutting themselves off from each other would limit their capacity to deliver far more than any restrictions arising from their participation in the EC would. It is the scale and stimulation provided by the EC that gives Europe's rich states the best hope for retaining that advanced industrial status needed for their high standards of living and public welfare.

The need to cooperate on this continental scale reflects the evolution of the world as a whole more than it does changes in Europe itself. In a global system with powers on the American, Soviet, or even Japanese scale, European states must operate as a bloc or expect to be dominated from without. Europe's growing solidarity is thus driven more by geopolitics than by any inner institutional logic or popular cultural transformation. Developing a more effective Community machinery or a broader European identity is the natural and necessary accompaniment to European cooperation. But these features are not themselves the primary autonomous driving force, which is geopolitical. They reinforce the geopolitical logic of cooperation, but they do not create it.

A geopolitical view, incidentally, should not discount the historical significance of the Community's institutional development. Those with a speculative turn of mind may well wonder if the Community's confederal system, with its politically more cohesive and administratively more efficient national units, may not eventually prove a better formula for running a continental political economy than the Soviet or even the American model. At the very least, the answer is not self-evident.

So far, western Europe has tried to increase its own economic and political cohesion, but without altering the hegemonic military arrangements with America. This policy is likely to prove self-defeating. The more the European states continue on their present confederal course, the more anomalous will seem their military dependency on America. Since a good part of their growing economic power will be felt in commercial confrontations, the United States is likely to grow more dissatisfied and assertive as its trade deficit resists quick improvement and its fiscal situation demands painful remedies. Europeans, caught up in the complexities of their own integration, and acutely conscious of their competitive vulnerabilities, will not take kindly to American demands for commercial concessions. American pressures will spill over to the military sphere, and Europeans will be pressed to relieve the United States of its excessive share of NATO's burdens. Since NATO costs now take up roughly half of the American defense budget, the substantial savings from cutting a significant portion of those forces would help bring the military budget under control and ease the rebalancing of American fiscal and monetary policy. But once their free ride is over, Europeans will grow more interested in designing and driving their own vehicle. In any event, the political as well as military requirements of a new European balance will encourage the western European coalition to extend itself to the military sphere.

Eastern Changes

While America's relative decline and western Europe's pragmatic consolidation have slowly been redefining roles in the trans-Atlantic relationship, the Soviet leg of the triangle has also become unstable. Many analysts are skeptical about the long-range prospects for Gorbachev's reforms. But few are unimpressed by his political skill, and some consider him a statesman of the first rank. He has jolted Soviet society from its complacent corruption and torpor. The new ferment of hope and discontent may penetrate to the foundations of the Soviet system. No one knows what will happen, nor is it easy to decide what would be desirable. A modernized political economy would make the Soviet Union more formidable, but might also make it more conscious of the benefits of interdependence and more assimilable into a peaceful and cooperative world system. Gorbachev's failure and a return to heavy-handed repression would provide intellectual relief to traditional Western analysts, but would not relieve the Soviet Union of its deep malaise and economic stagnation. In any event, a return to reaction in Russia could not restore the bipolar world. It would not reverse the trend to a more plural international system. It would not cure the American fiscal or balance-of-payments deficits, nor eliminate the need for America's geopolitical consolidation and Europe's greater military self-sufficiency.

The prospect that Gorbachev might fail to halt the Soviet decline suggests troubling historical precedents. One is Russia as a latter-day Ottoman Empire—its disintegration inciting quarrels among newly liberated peoples and among Europe's other great powers. Another is Russia as a latter-day Austria-Hungary, a regime wracked by internal discord and inclined to foreign interventions to bolster domestic prestige. The pan-Slav adventurism of the Romanov regime after 1905 is, perhaps, an even more appropriate analogy in the same vein.

In their crude versions, such analogies seem too apocalyptic. Implications of an East-West military confrontation seem fanciful. New Soviet interventions in eastern Europe, however, are not so improbable. The region is deeply agitated by frustrated nationalist ambitions and the accumulated failures of incompetent and heavy-handed communist regimes. But in a nuclear world Western armies are unlikely to march to the rescue. A far more probable reaction would be a rejuvenated NATO and reinvigorated popular interest in western European military cooperation.

Even these more restrained expectations seem excessive. They appear to assume that no one in Europe has learned anything since the 1950s. Should new and more liberal eastern European regimes evolve, they will most likely be extremely cautious about provoking a particularly irritable and distracted Russian Bear. Eastern European publics will be unlikely to push their leaders to suicidal extremes. Western European governments, moreover, will offer them no encouragement to do so. If eastern Europe goes through latter-day versions of the revolutions of 1848, western European governments are more likely to sympathize with the departing Metternichs than with the rising Mazzinis.

Gorbachev's success could easily pose a more serious challenge than his failure. Here again, extreme scenarios are common. A more liberal Soviet sphere could, it is feared, incite headlong Western competition for Eastern business that could destabilize not only eastern Europeans themselves, but also the EC. The rush of West German business interests to Czechoslovakia in 1968, for example, greatly annoyed the French and led to bitter recriminations after the Soviet intervention. In many people's minds, the principal danger today lies in a revival of Europe's perennial German problem. The possibility of an eastern Europe dominated by German finance and industry would please none of Germany's neighbors—to the east or to the west. And German reunification within a reborn centralized Reich would be no more popular today than it was earlier in the postwar era.

Again, these fears assume that no one has learned anything from Europe's past mistakes. There are, however, grounds for greater optimism. Recent chancellors of the Federal Republic have regularly disclaimed any ambition for a centralized form of German reunification. Rather, they hope for a confederal relationship within some broader pan-European system—a sort of extended European Community. A loosely confederal system is, after all, typical of German historical experience, save for the disastrous episode from 1870 to 1945. Even hopes for a formal confederation may be mostly rhetorical. The real aim, many argue, is a liberal evolution of the GDR's living conditions and human rights to the point where they no longer constitute such an egregiously painful contrast with Western standards. An "Austrian" outcome for East Germany would then have a powerful political logic—supported by major elements in West and East Germany, as well as the two superpowers and all of Germany's neighbors.

The apocalyptic historical analogies also discount western Europe's own collective evolution. By now, the European Community has given the Western states, including the Federal Republic, a commercial as well as political stake in west European integration vastly greater than anything that may reasonably be expected from an opening to the East. The intimate western European cooperation exemplified in the goals of 1992 would extend itself naturally to regulating competition over eastern European markets. Eastern European governments should themselves be leery of too vigorous a capitalist incursion, or too exclusive a dependence on West Germany. Commercial and financial limitations are likely, in any case, to reinforce political caution. It will take a long period of peaceful social and economic progress, and a great deal of capital, before eastern Europe or the Soviet Union can become genuine participants in some pan-European economy.

If Eastern economies begin moving in this direction, trans-Atlantic tensions are to be expected. Americans who see relations with the Soviet Union as a zero-sum contest for global hegemony feel threatened by any East-West trade that improves Soviet technological and industrial capacity. Most western European governments, if wary of Soviet military power, do not see their relationship locked forever in such implacable hostility. Instead, they believe the Soviets can be coaxed into a more interdependent and cooperative system. Their fundamental strategy is to promote an improvement in Eastern economic and political conditions at a rate that steers between stagnation and explosive change. In the end, they hope to see a "Europe from the Atlantic to the Urals." By this, they mean not Soviet hegemony but a balanced pan-European system.

Dangers of a Plural Europe: Finlandization?

The vision of a plural and balanced Europe is undoubtedly vague compared with the simplicities of the cold war. But its elements are not so difficult to imagine, and have not changed since de Gaulle first began articulating his vision of "Europe from the Atlantic to the Urals" after World War II. De Gaulle saw, on one side, a western European bloc built around a Franco-German partnership. It would be an ally but not a dependency of the United States. On the other side he saw a Soviet Union whose regime had become civilized away from the barbarities of Stalinism and constrained by the rise of powerful states in Asia. In the middle he saw an eastern Europe that had regained its independence and was acting as a buffer. Thus transformed, Europe's East and West could evolve from stupid confrontation into wary but fruitful collaboration.

De Gaulle's vision was that of a "realist" rather than a "utopian." There was no assumption of effortless, unarmed harmony. Instead, collaboration was to depend on an elaborate balance of the national interests of Europeans, Russians, and Americans. In particular, there was to be a powerful western European bloc. If the prospects now are that something like his vision will take recognizable form, what are the dangers?

The United States has traditionally feared western Europe's finlandization. In this scenario, endemic western European weakness combines with unquenchable Soviet ambition. America "loses" western Europe to the Soviets. Both the Atlantic alliance and western European solidarity break down before the power and blandishments of the East. With even a loose hegemony over Europe, the Russians will be able to control or extract the capital and technology needed to achieve the global status that has always been their national and ideological goal.

In effect, the scenario for finlandization faithfully reflects the bipolar perspective typical of postwar American geopolitical thinking. At the heart of American fears lies the presumption that western Europe's states are too gullible, weak, and divided to sustain an intimate relationship with the Soviet Union without falling under its domination. How realistic is this presumption?

Throughout the postwar era, these European states have shared a fear of Soviet military power, an aversion to Soviet political culture, and a contempt for Soviet economic backwardness. Nor has there been any lack of suspicion among them about Soviet predilections and motives. The real question is whether these same states have the will and the means to sustain their independence in the more balanced relationship with America and the Soviet Union implied in the vision of a more plural Europe.

The question bears upon both trans-Atlantic and western European arrangements. In effect, three issues intersect: Can the trans-Atlantic alliance hold together if the Soviet threat seems to go away? Can the western European coalition hold together in the face of an open eastern Europe and perhaps Soviet Union? And, in particular, can the Franco-German relationship persist in the face of apparently improved prospects for German national reunification?

Each of these questions has military, political, and economic dimensions. Each has its own particular calculations, although the answers are necessarily interdependent. On the military side, prospects are bound up with whether the western European states can rise adequately to an eventual American devolution within NATO. Western European powers do have the military resources to sustain a military balance, even if a policy of devolution significantly reduces the American contribution. Until now, Britain and France have used the American protectorate to husband their own military means. This reflects their assessment of where to invest their resources in order to serve their national interests, rather than any lack of concern about their security. Both, in fact, spend more on defense, proportionately, than the Federal Republic. An American devolution in NATO would obviously change their calculations on whether to emphasize European or global prowess.

The military requirements of European defense are anyway not as formidable as is often supposed. The upgraded British and French nuclear forces would be sufficient to provide a substantial European deterrent, provided an arrangement could be made to cover the Federal Republic and NATO's other non-nuclear powers. Obviously, European deterrence would be more credible in parallel with continuing American deterrence, which would itself be enhanced by some parallel European force. In other words, devolution could strengthen deterrence all around. Similarly, should Europeans desire a more convincing conventional balance as a result of changing strategic and political factors, they have the capacity to augment conventional strength very substantially. Indeed, a serious French commitment is the essential precondition for any serious conventional balance. Significant Soviet cuts would, of course, make the task substantially easier and might permit a much broader use of reserve and militia forces.

As the European Community indicates, western Europeans also have ample experience in organizing and administering cooperative arrangements among themselves. Politically, managing a military coalition is relatively uncomplicated compared with the intricate process of economic integration—a process that touches almost every domestic interest group and thus enters deeply into domestic politics.

In short, Europe's major states have never ceased to be concerned about their military security. They have the means necessary to preserve it, although they no doubt would prefer to have the Americans do it for them. There is no reason to suppose they would rather place themselves at the mercy of Soviet goodwill than give a military dimension to their already elaborate institutionalized cooperation. For Americans to assume that Europe's states will grow heedless of a military balance seems more a projection of past American isolationist attitudes onto the Europeans rather than a realistic assessment of Europe's own likely behavior.

The greatest fear is that the Soviets can detach the Federal Republic from its Western allies, especially France. As earlier sections of this chapter indicate, I believe the fears about Germany have been greatly exaggerated. The Federal Republic has for 30 years been building a European Community. Successive governments have clearly and deliberately chosen this European priority over national reunification. Whenever the issue has been posed seriously, the voting public has supported the European priority overwhelmingly. West German governments would truely prefer an Austrian solution for the GDR, at most within a loose confederal structure—and preferably European rather than German. The principal encouragement for German neutralism has been the assumption, entertained from time to time on the German left and perhaps less openly on the Atlanticist right, that the U.S. military protectorate would continue to provide security even if the Germans distanced themselves from NATO, the EC and France. The best cure for that illusion, never predominant in any case, is a firm American commitment to devolution.

Another widespread fear is that economic competition for Eastern favors will shatter Western cohesion. The West Germans are the principal object of this apprehension too—which, again, seems highly exaggerated. For the western Europeans, trade in the East is marginal compared to their mutual trade with each other. The trade figures in Table 1 give some indication. From this data it is difficult to imagine any calculation of economic interest that would persuade the West Germans to trade their western European partners for an adventure in the East. Once more, the main danger arises from the assumption that both are possible because the Americans will always under-

Table 1
Percentage of Overall Trade

Country of origin	Trade with United States		Trade with Soviet Union Eastern Europe		Trade with EC	
	M	X	M	X	M	X
West Germany	6.3	9.5	4.8	4.4	52.6	52.7
Britain	9.9	14.3	1.8	1.6	51.8	48.0
France	7.5	7.4	3.4	2.3	59.7	57.9
Italy	5.7	10.7	4.1	2.9	55.4	53.6
Netherlands	7.9	4.7	2.3	1.3	63.9	74.9
EC total	7.3	9.3	3.2	2.5	55.1	57.1
United States	—	—	0.5	0.9	20.5	24.5

M = Imports   X = Exports

Source: Organization for Economic Cooperation and Development, *Monthly Statistics on Foreign Trade* (December 1988).

write western European security. And once more, the cure is a firm American policy of devolution.

Trade figures alone show the overwhelming economic stake that EC members have in each other, but they seriously understate trans-Atlantic economic relationships. The giant Eurocurrency market gives some indication of the scale of such relationships. Huge reciprocal direct and indirect investments tie Europe and America together. The manufacturing product of these direct investments greatly exceeds the trans-Atlantic trade flows. (See Table 2.)

Table 2
Direct and Indirect Investment Position
of the United States and Western Europe
at the End of 1986
(Millions of dollars)

Type of investment	Western Europe in United States	United States in western Europe
Direct	141,669	123,183
Indirect	409,652	219,494

Source: Survey of Current Business (June 1987), p. 39.

In the long run, of course, it may be different. Economic, social, and cultural patterns obviously can and do change. Parts of eastern Asia have industrialized and developed an enormous American trade within two or three decades. Something similar may be improbable in Europe, but who can say that it is impossible? The question is whether the United States should automatically see such a development as a threat. From the bipolar geopolitical perspective of the cold war, the answer tends to be yes. But can America remain stuck with a policy for Europe that counts on the failure of Soviet liberalization?

American Vision

America's initial policy for the postwar world reflected a different vision. A liberal world economy was to replace the protectionist confrontations of the 1930s with a competitive but peaceful interdependence leading to mutual gain. The rival autarkies of prewar Britain, Germany, Japan, and the Soviet Union were to disappear into a new global system that would promote trade and economic prosperity, rather than war and ruin.

Since the cold war, America's bipolar and liberal perspectives have grown entwined and confused. Yet the bipolar geopolitical perspective has never entirely eclipsed the liberal. Most of the time, and throughout most of the world, American policy has sought to create and sustain a liberal global order. The classic rationale holds that such an order is more humane, more efficient, and more peaceful. Liberal rights safeguard individual freedom and dignity. The free market encourages a division of labor that maximizes the welfare of all participants. Free trade leads to efficient but peaceful competition and interdependence.

No doubt the original rationale was a bit simpleminded. But the postwar era has added macroeconomic management, the welfare state, and a panoply of interstate organizations, including the European Community itself. The extraordinary development of the world economy during the *Pax Americana* has given this refined version of global liberalism a great practical success. Human rights and free markets do form a system, it seems, that not only is more humane and agreeable, but also appears to work much better. The terrible sacrifices made to the illiberal ideas of fascism and communism turn out to have been not only morally indefensible, but also economically mistaken.

From the liberal perspective, however, so long as the postwar liberal world economy remains in place, opening eastern European and Soviet economies ought not to be a threat but a great opportunity. Trade and investment connections in one area are not supposed to grow at the expense of those in another.

Granted, a liberal system requires a political and military foundation. Today's great historical issue is whether the liberal world economy can survive America's declining hegemony. Can a global liberal economic system coexist with a plural geopolitical system? Why not? Hegemony, after all, is not the only way to organize political order. Many domestic and regional systems, including our own federal Constitution, are based on the ancient notion of a balance of power.

Theorists will probably go on debating the abstract advantages of benevolent hegemony versus those of a pluralist balance of power until the end of history itself. The most practical view is that either system will work if the conditions are right. What will not work is to insist on one system when conditions require another. When conditions no longer favor hegemony, a policy that either insists on sustaining it or expects to continue free-riding on it becomes a formula for national and systemic disaster.

These global speculations are central to the future of the American-European-Soviet triangular relationship. If the global economy breaks down in general recrimination, the drift toward a world of blocs will greatly intensify. In such an environment, zero-sum calculations of national interest will prevail. The liberal West will endure severe pressures and dislocations in its own trans-Atlantic core. In a world of protectionist blocs the possibility of European-Soviet accommodations at America's expense are not as fanciful as might be wished. In any event, if the West cannot rebalance its economic and military relations, the deteriorating prospects for the liberal world economy point to an infinity of future troubles.

If, on the other hand, Europe and America can rebalance their own relations, prospects for a successful evolution of triangular relations are not unpromising. A militarily more self-sufficient western European bloc means not only a more stable Atlantic system, but also better prospects for a stable European system. No one knows what Gorbachev's grand initiatives will bring to the Soviet sphere. But a West with its own affairs in order ought to be able to accommodate any new Russia and discourage any revival of the old.

An internally more successful Soviet Union slowly brought into a liberal and cooperative world system will be a much greater gain for the world than a loss for U.S.–European ties. Transatlantic commercial, financial, and industrial relations will probably always remain the major link in an interdependent world economy. The deep cultural and societal affinities between America and Europe will persist, while the contrasting trans-Atlantic fashions and experiments will continue to challenge and energize both sides. But a more liberal, satisfied, and humane Soviet Union could make its own contribution. The triangular relationship of America, Europe, and Russia might take on a more natural and creative stability than it had in the bipolar past. The European system might cease to be the cockpit of global rivalry and become instead the keystone of an enduring global peace.

Notes

1. In the period 1970–1985, France and West Germany increased their defense spending (in 1980 prices) by 12 percent and 21 percent, respectively, while the United States cut spending by 32 percent. In 1975–1980, all three registered increases—France, 24 percent, and West Germany and the United States, 6 percent each. See *NATO Review*, No. 6 (December 1988), p. 30.
2. International Monetary Fund, *World Economic Outlook* (Washington, D.C., April 1989), p. 75.

3. Organization of Economic Cooperation and Development (OECD), *Historical Statistics 1960–1986* (Paris, 1988), p. 61; International Monetary Fund, *World Economic Outlook* (Washington, D.C., April 1989), p. 69.

A New Europe, A Renewed Atlantic Link

Robert D. Hormats

The winds of change in Europe, once only a mild breeze, are now reaching gale force. Increasing economic strength and unity in western Europe, coupled with the rejection of doctrinaire communism in the Soviet Union and much of eastern Europe, present enormous opportunities for a more secure, humane, and democratic European continent—while posing great opportunities and challenges for U.S.–European relations.

A Basis for Optimism

The western Europeans have become the chief architects building the new Europe to replace the divided one forged in the ashes of World War II and hardened during the cold war. The future shape of Europe will turn on whether the European Community (EC) can accomplish two tasks in the decade ahead: one, to generate centrifugal forces in eastern Europe strong enough to draw reform-minded nations there more clearly into its economic and political orbit, without threatening Moscow to the point that it intervenes to reverse the process; two, to create centripetal forces in western Europe strong enough that West Germans will see any future association between their country and East Germany as taking place in a Community context. If it can achieve these objectives, the EC by virtue of its moral, political, and social—as well as economic—strength will be well positioned to form the foundation on which any future "common European home" will be built.

U.S.–European economic, political, and security relationships are bound to come under greater scrutiny in the 1990s. Western Europe now insists on a stronger voice on global economic matters and on NATO (North Atlantic Treaty Organization) security affairs, and will continue to do so in the years ahead. American and European differences over trade and other economic issues will raise a series of problems, and U.S. perceptions of Europe's security interests and Europeans' perceptions of their own interests will likely diverge. Debate and, perhaps, conflict loom not only over issues such as the modernization of tactical nuclear weapons, but also over curbs on technology exports to the Soviet Union, strategy in arms control negotiations, the degree of verification necessary to make treaties credible, defense burden sharing, and weapons procurement. Friction also could arise over regional issues in such areas as the Middle East and Central America.

As the western Europeans strike a more independent posture, Washington will be increasingly uncomfortable with the challenges this poses to its leadership. The widely held perception of a major Soviet threat, which for much of the postwar period served as the cementing force for NATO and as a basis to rally popular support in the West for large expenditures on sophisticated weaponry, has diminished. That same threat also contained economic differences among Western nations; it created a compelling argument for compromising potentially divisive trade and monetary issues to preserve alliance unity. As fear of the Soviets has declined, so has popular support for NATO, for financing expensive new weapons and for maintaining current nuclear arsenals. Antinuclear sentiment is particularly strong in West Germany, which plays a pivotal role in the forward defense strategy of the alliance. Much of Gorbachev's public relations effort, it should be noted, is aimed not primarily at winning the support of American and western Europeans but rather at loosening the Federal Republic's commitment to NATO and convincing West German citizens that a strong nuclear deterrent is unneccesary.

Nor will invoking the cause of alliance unity serve to induce economic compromise. A more assertive European Community trade policy (and, at times, perhaps a more restrictive one) leading up to 1992, combined with tougher U.S. measures under the 1988 Trade Act, is likely to lead to periods of trans-Atlantic friction. These developments could sharpen American sentiment for unilateral troop reductions in Europe. Such pressure is likely to grow also because of U.S. budgetary constraints, concerns about large trade deficits, and questions about allied burden sharing—although President Bush's arms negotiation proposals at the NATO summit in May 1989 should alleviate such pressure for a while.

By the year 2000, however, the United States will likely have accommodated western Europe's desire for greater independence of economic and political action and for significant progress in reducing East-West tension on the continent. Western Europe, in turn, will likely have accommodated America's desire that the European members of NATO assume greater responsibility for their own defense and for the global economy. Assuming a continued, if perhaps somewhat attenuated, Western consensus on security strategy, the alliance will continue to field a viable military force. It will continue to rely to a large degree on an American strategic deterrent, even though a Strategic Arms Reduction Talks (START) treaty may well be reached in the interim, but the strategic nuclear capabilities of Britain and France will play a more prominent role than they have in the 1980s.

Before the century's end NATO and the Warsaw Pact are likely to have negotiated asymmetrical troop cuts as part of a package in which Moscow also commits to deploy its armored weaponry in a basically defensive posture. If they succeed, there will be fewer U.S. troops in Europe. Western European nations will probably cut their troop levels and reduce their military budgets as a percentage of their gross national product; having done so they will seek to enhance their collective defense capabilities and sustain their commitments to NATO by engaging more actively in cooperative weapons research and production ventures and intensify collaborative efforts among their armed forces. The United States and its allies will also expand the scope and definition of security cooperation to include preservation of the environment, combating terrorism, and drug interdiction to broaden NATO's peacetime appeal and increase its relevance to the "successor generation."

This is an optimistic outlook, one that—to paraphrase Dr. Pangloss in *Candide*—is the best of all possible U.S.–European relationships that can be expected as we enter the next millennium. It is predicated on the notion that powerful forces on both sides of the now-rusting Iron Curtain are at work to eliminate division in Europe, to pursue security at a lower cost and lower level of tension, and to devote more resources to domestic economic goals and less to defense. I shall attempt to justify this optimism further in the pages that follow.

However, the current environment of promise and optimism is vulnerable to three major threats. The first would be a major blowup in eastern Europe, or one of the Baltic states, due to an outburst of nationalism or intense dissatisfaction with economic conditions. That could thwart the process of negotiating troop reductions, cause an abrupt hardening of attitudes in the Soviet Union toward normalization with the West, and undermine both glasnost and perestroika. Internal developments in the Soviet Union, similar to those in China in 1989 challenging the very authority of the communist party, could have similar effects, leading to a reversal of Gorbachev's policies or possibly even his removal.

The second threat would be a turn toward protectionism by either the European Community or the United States that would weaken economic cooperation and strengthen pressure for unilateral action on political as well as security matters.

The third threat would be a global recession that could lead weaker companies in western Europe to seek a slowdown or halt in the removal of internal barriers, associated with the creation of the 1992 Single Market, which leave them vulnerable to competition from companies within the Community. A world recession would also hurt exports of nations in the Soviet bloc, where economies are already in a precarious situation.

In this period of potentially dramatic change, western Europeans and Americans will need constantly to remind themselves that, although their policies will likely diverge on a greater number of issues, a fundamental and durable source of their international economic and political influence—and certainly of their security—is their close relationship with one another.

Both sides of the Atlantic will need to keep that point in sharp perspective lest the forces of change obscure it.

Europe's Challenge, America's Stakes

Western Europe is now challenged by its own postwar economic success. It has enjoyed peace and stability under NATO. And it is a prime beneficiary of Moscow's now less-threatening posture. The Community is moving energetically to dismantle impediments to the movement of goods, people, capital, and services among member nations—a process that many regard as establishing the basis for greater western European political unity, a more sharply defined European voice in international affairs, and a larger role for Europeans in their own defense.

A debate is emerging in Europe over how to exert greater authority on the world stage. One school of thought— advanced, among others, by members of the Social Democratic Party in West Germany and the Labour Party in Britain—holds that the Soviet Union and western Europe can reconcile most of their ideological and political differences very quickly. This line opposes new expenditures for nuclear weaponry and supports significantly intensified East-West trade and financial relations. It argues that improved East-West ties will make it possible to achieve Charles de Gaulle's dream of "a Europe from the Atlantic to the Urals" or, at a minimum, to tear down barriers to the movement of people and dramatically reduce tensions. Western Europe, the argument continues, should loosen its military and political links to the United States—which are pointed to as an abnormal legacy of the cold war—and "Europeanize" its own security. An extreme version of this argument holds that western Europe should quickly denuclearize and distance itself from Washington on security matters in order to hasten the process of intra-European normalization.

Another, more centrist, school advances a very different vision—one of a western Europe that, while asserting more control over its own economic and political future, and pursuing closer economic and political ties with the East, remains firmly a part of the Atlantic alliance and militarily well prepared, with a credible nuclear deterrent. This vision is based on the view that NATO's unity and its defense capability must be preserved even as relations with the Soviets improve; indeed, Western strength and NATO cohesion are seen as a prerequisite for success in future arms reduction talks with Moscow, and are in any case needed because the long-term outlook for Soviet policy is still unclear. Moreover, the argument continues, the alliance provides western Europe protection enabling it to concentrate on strengthening its internal economic cohesion.

Whichever version of Europe emerges will not be the product of an American vision but of the confluence of political, economic, and social forces in Europe itself. Yet the stakes for the United States are high. America's international power and influence are heavily dependent on its alliances with western Europe and Japan. West Germany's role as an American ally in NATO is particularly vital to the balance of power on the continent and to the West's ability to exert influence in central Europe.

But American policy cannot be predicated on the assumption that the postwar status quo will last indefinitely, that western Europe will accept permanent animosity with the Soviet Union or eastern Europe, or that America's allies will not increasingly seek to assert their self-identity in international affairs—often in ways that differentiate them from the United States. Yet global stability and European security continue to depend heavily on the United States. Washington will need to walk a fine line between maintaining a sufficient deterrent capability in Europe to be credible in Moscow, and encouraging other NATO members to do likewise, while avoiding the charge that it is somehow blocking progress in reducing armaments and tensions on the continent. Still, no country today can challenge America's combination of military power, wealth, and political authority—and no other nation would be able to play the role of "replacement power" should America's global influence weaken significantly, as the United States did when Britain's power declined earlier in this century.

Three constraints will be important in shaping Europe's

course over the next decade. First, western Europe's strategic options are limited by global power relationships. Western Europe has a superpower, the Soviet Union, on its continent. As western Europe itself is not a superpower, it must depend on the world's other superpower, its ally the United States, to counter Soviet influence and Soviet armies. As long as there is even a potential Soviet threat—and there will be one, notwithstanding Gorbachev's encouraging announcements of unilateral force cuts in eastern Europe, as long as Soviet military forces remain large and offensively postured, and Moscow's political and military domination continues in eastern Europe—America's defense commitment and its military presence will remain vital to western Europe's security and to its ability to resist pressures from Moscow.

A second limit relates to international economic options. European prosperity is inextricably intertwined with that of the United States and other major trading nations in and outside of Europe. Expanding trade within the European Community clearly will be the most important stimulus to growth in members nations. Trade will also grow between the EC and the nations of the European Free Trade Association—Sweden, Finland, Austria, Norway, Switzerland, and Iceland—which together are the EC's largest outside trading partner. And there will doubtless be benefits in increasing trade with eastern Europe, as part of the political and economic normalization process. However, the United States will remain by far the most important offshore commercial and financial partner for western Europe. And the Far East will be both a formidable competitor and a growing market for European goods. Alliances with American, Asian, and other European companies will abound as European firms work to build economies of scale, engage in cooperative research to share costs, and seek quick delivery of newly developed products to global markets.

Thus, while western Europe strengthens its internal economic unity, the importance of its links with the rest of the world will limit its ability to turn inward. In short, a "Fortress Europe" is not a viable option. The ultimate test of the Community's economic reforms will be their success in helping companies in member countries better meet foreign competition in an open global economy—not in insulating them from it—and in putting those companies in a position to negotiate alliances with large foreign firms on the basis of equality.

A third limit is internal. A unified western European economy will require the support of a strong intra-European political consensus. It cannot sweep aside the need for bargains among independent sovereign states; in that regard, the analogy of a "United States of Europe" is flawed. The American states did not embody distinctly separate nationalities with ancient languages, cultures, histories, and institutions. The nations of Europe do. Such distinctions remain important, although they have not stood in the way of progress and need not inhibit it in the future. Further progress in tearing down internal economic impediments will depend more on how credible the process seems to the electorates in individual nations than on whether the idea conforms to a particular economic or bureaucratic model, however ideal.

A broad political consensus will be required to sustain the momentum of integration. Technicians can take the process only so far. But political support can no longer be bought by subsidies or protection. Membership in the Community means that each nation has agreed to take a broader vision of its interests and to relinquish the use of these tools vis-à-vis its neighbors. Years of attempting to preserve protected and highly regulated national economies have lead to competitive weakness and high unemployment in western Europe, while Canada, Japan, and the United States have surged technologically and have succeeded in generating millions of new jobs.

Virtually all else that western Europe hopes to accomplish over the rest of this century at home and abroad will depend on its success in building a unified and more efficient Single Market that generates new jobs, accelerates social progress, and enables Europeans to engage more fully in the global technological revolution. That would also establish a stronger basis for western Europe to increase its role in its own defense and to reduce tensions with eastern Europe. This process will be particularly important to retain and enhance the tight integration between West Germany and the rest of western Europe.

Establishing a single internal market by 1992 will hardly be a smooth process. But whether it is achieved by 1992 or after 2000 is not a crucial issue. The process of tearing down internal barriers is well and wisely under way; it may slow from time to time in coming years, but it can be reversed only at great cost. By the end of this century, if all goes reasonably according to plan, western Europe will be a far more efficient economic entity than it is today—with a larger number of world-class companies capable of going head-to-head with competitors abroad. These companies will not necessarily be exclusively European in ownership or location, but their European components are likely to be in a stronger position in global corporate alliances owing to the Single Market.

The Role of European Institutions

It is inevitable that within western Europe, more power and influence will shift from national capitals to European Community institutions. Although this will involve a transfer of a measure of sovereignty, world economic conditions—specifically, the rapid rise in global economic interdependence and an even higher degree of interdependence within western Europe—already imply a diminution of sovereignty. Governments cannot hope to promote prosperity at home in isolation. The fundamental economic goals of western European nations now must be attained by pooling their efforts in the context of the Community. Narrow or short-term national objectives need to be suppressed to accomplish longer-term objectives of scale, efficiency, and stable growth.

By the year 2000 the European Commission will have assumed a greater regulatory role on subjects such as mergers, the environment and government subsidies. But as its role increases, it will come under greater scrutiny by the European Council, composed of ministers of national governments, and the European Parliament, directly elected by voters in member

nations. The Council and Parliament will, like national governments, constantly debate whether western Europe should
structure its integrated economy along socialist, social democratic, liberal, or conservative lines. But the worst examples of
government regulation at the national level—which were en-
acted when heavy regulation was fashionable and which have
survived through inertia even as their costs have become
increasingly burdensome—are not likely to be replicated as
Europe creates new rules from a fresh start. Political leaders,
such as Margaret Thatcher, are likely to see to it that as the
Commission assumes more power it does not replicate the mistakes of national governments; indeed, the Commission itself
shows no signs of wanting to do this.

Particularly controversial is the idea of creating a European
central bank. It is favored by those who believe that the decision
to eliminate capital controls by all members of the Community
by 1992 requires a central bank to manage monetary policy.
They also assert that over time a common currency, under a
European central bank, will be required to avoid trade distor-
tions that result from the exchange rate fluctuations to which
western Europe would continue to be vulnerable if it retained
separate currencies.

Creating a central bank and a common currency will be difficult, however. One frequently cited model is the U.S. Federal
Reserve. But the Fed makes decisions based on inputs from
regional governors, who have considerable influence, and is
responsive (although not beholden) to a nationwide political
and financial constituency. In Europe today, monetary policy
and the European Monetary System are heavily influenced
by—and, indeed, borrow credibility from—the highly regarded
anti-inflationary policy of the German Bundesbank, which other national banks follow to varying degrees. If a genuine European central bank is to be created, it will need to command
legitimacy from Dublin to Rome so that it can operate without
excessive political interference.

Moreover, equilibrating mechanisms are as yet lacking in
Europe. With separate currencies, if one country is suffering
from a trade deficit, its currency can decline, thereby boosting

net exports. With a single currency, other means of achieving equilibrium must be found. One strength of the very diverse American economy, with its single currency, is that when disparities in trade or economic activity exist among regions of the country, labor can move relatively easily from one area to another where customs and language are the same; and income is transferred within the country as federal tax receipts from states experiencing slow growth decline while federal benefits to people in those states increase. Such processes do not yet exist in western Europe.

In the next decade it is likely that the European Community will create a central bank roughly equivalent in structure to the U.S. Federal Reserve System, but with more limited powers. Already EC Commission President Jacques Delors has put forward a creative and comprehensive blueprint for a European monetary system. The European Currency Unit (ECU) will be utilized more extensively for denominating commercial transactions and financing governments, corporations, and entities such as the European Development Fund. The ECU will also become a parallel currency within the Community, although by 2000 it probably will not yet displace national currencies.

Nevertheless, as the ECU's role in global finance and monetary affairs becomes more prevalent and substantial, it will have profound effects on the international monetary system, thereby requiring the United States and other countries to consider whether changes in that system are needed. Indeed, it would be wise to begin studying possible reform in the international monetary system in parallel with the EC's exercise to reform its internal system. By design and by the sheer magnetism of its economic pull, the Community—in its own right and as a result of a panopoly of new trade arrangements which it is likely to negotiate—will become a formidable trading force over the remainder of this century and will be able to use foreign access to its market as a powerful lever to obtain access for its products to other world markets.

Up to a point, utilizing economic strength to obtain trading advantages is a legitimate tactic. But taken to excess, it would lead to conflict between western Europe and its key trading partners—particularly the United States. That in turn could weaken NATO security ties if Americans—alarmed by threats to their commercial interests—insist that Washington threaten to withdraw troops from western Europe in retaliation or to force concessions from the Community.

The current Uruguay Round of multilateral trade negotiations is, in this respect, of critical importance. The earlier Kennedy Round was launched at the beginning of the 1960s to cut worldwide tariff levels, in part to keep the then newly formed European Economic Community from turning inward. The current round can do likewise if its major players—the United States, Japan, EC Europe, Canada, Australia, and a number of major Third World nations—are willing collectively to commit themselves to reduce the myriad of nontariff barriers that distort international commerce.

For the Community this means negotiating agreements that open more of its industries to competition from outside (in return, of course, for similar measures by its trading partners), just as they are being exposed to intensified competition from within Europe by the 1992 process. Community industries that are used to high levels of protection or subsidies will bitterly resist. EC members might be tempted to fashion compromises that assist industries being hurt by additional competition from within Europe by declining to open further their market to non-EC competition, or by shielding European producers temporarily from non-European goods.

If Europe is perceived by Americans as resisting progress in the Uruguay Round or creating new barriers to outside competition, Washington will find itself besieged by domestic pressures to take tough trade measures against Europe—even if for broader political and security reasons it prefers not to do so. That would also give impetus to the creation of competing trading groups—in the Western Hemisphere and among nations on the Pacific Rim. Even though those groups would probably be less formally organized than the Community, they could constrain western Europe's global trading opportunities.

A similar danger would be Washington's overly aggressive use of provisions in the 1988 Trade Act. That could drive the Community to impose new restrictions of its own in retaliation, and generate pressures for the EC to utilize its growing economic cohesion to counter American pressure. The net result would be that trade disputes could drive a wedge between Europe and America on political and security matters.

Trade disputes over agriculture, government procurement, services, and telecommunications are likely from time to time in the next decade as Europe's Single Market evolves and as America's 1988 Omnibus Trade Act is assertively implemented. By the close of the next decade, however, it is likely that Europe and the United States will have reached understandings that put most major trade differences behind them or at least permitted them to be resolved in an orderly fashion.

Overcoming the Divided Continent

In coming years the Community, which already has trade agreements with many of its neighbors, is likely to negotiate new agreements with a broader range of countries. While the Community is putting in place the directives and rules that together form the basis for the Single Market, it will not accept new members. After that, pressures will grow to do so; certainly Austria and Turkey will push hard. The risk perceived in the Community, however, is that the entrance of new members in the next several years could overburden the EC apparatus. There is also resistance in some EC members to admission of low-wage countries on grounds that this would give unfettered access to low-cost goods in their markets, thereby costing jobs and profits, and causing their economies to be flooded by "cheap labor." And there is concern that when the subject of new members arises it would force the Community to confront the question of whether including nations that are neutral by treaty or by long-standing policy (as opposed to Ireland, which is now a member) would prevent the Community from becoming a political and security union as envisaged by the Treaty of Rome. Alternatively, the EC would have to work out arrangements so that neutrals such as Austria could join and cooperate fully on economic matters, while remaining outside of Community political and security collaboration.

By the end of this century there are likely to be relatively few full new members in the Community. Far more numerous will be nations associated by arrangements of various types. Agreements are likely to be negotiated establishing free-trade ties with Switzerland and Finland, as well as with Austria if it is not permitted to join, and with Mediterranean countries such as Cyprus and Malta. These agreements can also enhance cooperation in other areas such as in investment, setting common product standards, and adopting similar types of labor standards. Still other agreements—for instance with eastern European nations and possibly the Soviet Union—will lead to trade expansion and liberalization on a more limited scale. The net result will be a widening map of trade and economic ties in Europe centered on the Community. In this way the Community could become the centerpiece around which any future "common European home" is built, and the arbiter of its rules.

It might be possible to envisage by the end of this century a Europe of concentric economic circles: one, the EC at its core; two, several neutrals and other nations in the Mediterranean enjoying particularly close commercial relations with, or associate membership in, the EC, which might also be invited to participate in regular consultations with the Commission, Council of Ministers, and committees of the European Parliament where their interests are directly at stake, but with no formal vote; three, some eastern European nations, and perhaps the Soviet Union itself, having arrangements with the EC permitting substantially increased two-way trade, along with investment treaties to encourage new and joint ventures. Associate membership might even be possible for those in the third category whose reforms over time lead their economies to operate largely on the basis of market forces.

Improving trade ties with eastern Europe will be a major western European enterprise of the 1990s. Although East-West trade is likely to remain a small percentage of total western

European trade, it can play an important role in supporting eastern Europe's economic reforms and reducing the dependence on the Soviet Union of a number of countries of the Council for Mutual Economic Assistance (COMECON). Moreover, for several years western Europe will find it difficult to increase its net exports to the United States, which will be in the process of reducing its enormous trade deficit; in fact, the EC's net exports to the American market are likely to decline. So increased exports to eastern Europe will be attractive even if large-scale trade financing is required to support them.

In recent years America and Europe frequently have differed over the pace and character of improvements in economic relations with the Soviet Union. In the early 1980s Washington worried that western Europe would become too dependent on the Soviet market or on its energy supplies and was too lax in selling the Soviets sophisticated technology that could provide benefits for their military. In 1982 Washington was especially critical of—and took serious action to stop—large, subsidized credits to Moscow for, among other things, a natural gas pipeline to the West.

In the fall of 1988, the United States expressed reservations about a spate of new European credits to the Soviet Union—even though these were reported to be on market terms and Washington was itself subsidizing agricultural sales to the Soviet Union. The American argument has been that large export credits will enable the Kremlin to meet the resource needs of the civilian sector without having to divert significant resources from the military or to undertake dramatic economic changes. Credit is thus seen as a substitute for, rather than an inducement to, economic reform.

In the short run, this issue may cause friction: suppose, for instance, that particular European technology sales seemed to the Pentagon to provide Moscow with military advantage. However, by the turn of the century this issue should be less troublesome. The course of perestroika will have become clearer. The West also should have a better idea of whether Soviet policies genuinely moderated or simply departed temporarily from the more traditional and threatening Soviet approach.

Lending to the Soviet Union and eastern Europe will take place in an environment of greater transparency.

Effective Western management of East-West economic relations will be important to harmony in the alliance. As the effort to normalize economic relations with socialist economies proceeds, the West must consider a pivotal question: on whose terms should that normalization take place? Because it is the West's approach to economic policy that has succeeded and the East's that has failed, arrangements that simply "split the difference" would be counterproductive. Extending large-scale credits to socialist nations, or allowing them to participate in global economic institutions without evidence of significant reform on their part, would be self-defeating. The West's goal should be to draw the Soviets and the eastern Europeans over time into the network of international, market-oriented economic relationships in support of, and in parallel with, domestic economic reforms in these nations. And it should maintain a strong consensus on ways to avoid—through the COCOM group of Western nations constituted to control technology transfer—sales of technology that could potentially benefit the Soviet military. In a similar spirit it should agree to avoid the provision of large-scale subsidized credits to the Soviet Union and the nations of eastern Europe.

Both President Bush and President Gorbachev have supported the goal of bringing the Soviet Union into the international economic system. Gorbachev dramatized this point in a letter to the Paris Economic Summit that stressed: "Our perestroika is inseparable from a policy aiming at our full participation in the world economy." Soviet membership in global institutions such as the General Agreement on Tariffs and Trade (GATT), the World Bank, and the International Monetary Fund (IMF) is inappropriate at the moment, but there are various ways in which experts in these institutions and the Soviet Union might increase their exchange of information on economic developments. This could permit Soviet officials to understand the practical consequences of normalization of economic and trade relations with the West, and the West to better understand how the Soviets would perform as members or observers in these institutions.

Observer status in the GATT should be considered just *after* the conclusion of the Uruguay Round. Addressing this now would divert attention from the round's negotiating goals. This, of course, assumes that internal reforms continue. Granting observer status need not imply a commitment to ultimate full membership. That should be a separate decision. In the meantime an active exchange of information and an organized set of consultations should take place to enhance Soviet understanding of the functioning of the trading system, help Moscow to design a tariff system consistent with the process of normalizing trade relations with market economies, and give the Kremlin a chance to dispel fears in the West that it would use membership to politicize the organization, as it has done with respect to the trade issue in the United Nations.

The World Bank and IMF have no equivalent to observer status in the GATT. But regular consultations among their experts and those of the Soviet Union could permit those institutions to obtain more information on the Soviet economy and its financing needs while enabling Soviet reformers to avail themselves of the expertise in these institutions on exchange rates, pricing, banking, and credit issues. In both cases, closer contacts will help Soviet officials to determine how to adjust their policies and practices to participate more effectively in the world economy. America and Europe need to work together to identify the optimal strategy and pace for integrating the Soviets into these types of arrangements and institutions.

Eastern Europe should be distinguished from the Soviet Union. Western Europe can utilize its economic strength to gradually draw individual nations of eastern Europe (recognizing the differences in their approach to economic reform) closer to it and away from Moscow, without threatening Soviet security relationships to the point that Moscow seeks to reverse the process. Indeed, the Kremlin might find closer economic ties between eastern and western Europe to be a way of reducing costly commitments of its own in eastern Europe and diffusing what could become an explosive situation should economic conditions in that region deteriorate.

The Community's unique advantage in this respect was recognized at the July 1989 economic summit in Paris. There, Chancellor Kohl and President Bush supported giving the EC Commission the lead in coordinating the effort to assist reform in eastern Europe and provide food aid to Poland. This action depoliticized the process vis-à-vis Moscow, and made it easier for eastern Europeans to accept the help without appearing to the Kremlin to be slipping into America's clutches. It also enabled West Germany to play a key role in eastern Europe within the context of the EC, countering concerns that the Federal Republic might be tempted to take unilateral economic or political initiatives in the region.

On another front, the Community and its members are begining to link loans to, and trade with, their socialist neighbors to efforts to lessen tensions and support reforms. In 1987 West German loans to Hungary were conditioned on the continuation of liberal reforms and increased cultural contacts between the two countries. In 1988 the French government announced its intention to link its roughly $2 billion in new credits to the Soviet Union to progress in reducing conventional arms in Europe; this avoids the inconsistency of providing the Soviets large amounts of money while Moscow continues to maintain massive conventional forces that require offsetting Western defense spending. In that same year the EC and COMECON signed a declaration of "mutual recognition." The Community insisted on and obtained two conditions—that West Berlin be treated as part of the EC and that future trade agreements be with *individual* COMECON nations, not with the Moscow-dominated COMECON organization itself.

The latter was a step toward loosening Moscow's economic grip on eastern Europe. Soon after, the Community reached a trade agreement with Hungary, eastern Europe's most market-oriented economy; the EC promised to phase out most of its quotas against Hungary, which agreed to provide easier access for Community businesses. More limited agreements were reached later with Czechoslovakia and Poland. The Soviet

Union and Bulgaria are seeking similar arrangements. But they are unlikely to receive as favorable treatment because their governments tightly control prices; and the absence of a credible, market-oriented price mechanism raises the chance that these nations will dump or heavily subsidize exports to the Community.

The Community approach to COMECOM nations is thus dual-tracked. It seeks to enable the nations of eastern Europe to regain their historical position as an integrated part of Europe in terms of human rights, freedom of movement, and democratic reforms, yet does not fully include them in the EC because their economies are not able to fully integrate with those of western Europe and still do not adhere to market principles. Moreover, they are, of course, still members of the Warsaw Pact.

Over time, in a more peaceful and less-armed Europe, Poland, Hungary, and Czechoslovakia should be able to resume, as closely as geopolitics permit, their positions as integral parts of Europe. By culture, religion, and history they can in no way be considered a logical part of the Soviet sphere of influence much less its empire. Ties between Paris and Warsaw, Prague and Berlin, and Vienna and Budapest are as much a part of the common European background as are the Renaissance or the Reformation. Trying to bring the two parts of Europe closer together responds to an historic urge which both sides feel. The historical basis of a "whole Europe," or "common house," it is worth recalling, goes back to the Empire of Charlemagne, and then the Holy Roman Empire, and should at a minimum encompass their territories.

Drawing Down Conventional Forces

Closer economic ties between western Europe and the COMECON nations are virtually inevitable in coming years, and differences of approach between western Europe and the United States are to be expected. However, these differences can be more easily accommodated within the alliance than can disputes over security issues. Normalizing security relationships between East and West will require a clear agreement within

NATO; strategic stability on the continent cannot be attained if Americans and western Europeans pursue separate strategies.

Here, as in economics, the central question is: on whose terms? A cohesive NATO alliance is a major source of strength for the West. Yet some western Europeans appear to believe that they will be more credible as an interlocutor with Moscow by holding the two superpowers equally responsible for the continuation of divisions on the continent. Others appear to have concluded that for budgetary or balance-of-payments reasons America soon will have to pull back from its extensive world security role, and thus argue that greater accommodation with Moscow is prudent "hedging" policy. Still others argue on moral grounds for unilaterally moving toward a nuclear-free western Europe.

These notions, if broadly embraced, encourage acceptance of the idea that more normal relations in Europe must be achieved to a substantial degree on Moscow's terms. The opposite is more accurate. Western democracies will be in a powerful position vis-à-vis Moscow for years to come. The Soviet Union and its allies need a respite from international tensions in order to achieve domestic economic priorities.

President Bush made the most of these circumstances at the NATO summit in 1989 by taking the initiative to offer proposals aimed at lowering Warsaw Pact and NATO force levels. In many respects the summit was a watershed, for it took the United States and its allies off the defensive in the competition with Gorbachev and demonstrated NATO resolve to link large conventional cuts to cuts in short-range nuclear weapons. It also, temporarily at least, diffused pressure in the United States for unilateral conventional force cuts in Europe.

The West's primary negotiating goal should be to press Gorbachev to make good on his own notions of "reasonable sufficiency" and a "defensive" military doctrine. It should seek a dismantling of a large portion of Soviet armor—tanks, mobile heavy artillery, and infantry fighting vehicles—together with dramatic cuts in the divisions Moscow now has forward-deployed in eastern Europe and stationed in its western military districts. Dismantling some of these forward-deployed divisions rather than simply redeploying them is important to avoid their being moved up to the front at some time in the future on short notice or being redeployed to Asia or the Caucasus.

As the United States has suggested, asymmetrical cuts in conventional forces should be a prerequisite for cuts in short-range nuclear weapons. The latter weapons then would not be required in such abundance by NATO because conventional cuts would make the Warsaw Pact far less able to launch a surprise attack and engage in massive offensive operations. If that goal can be attained, and if effective verification procedures can be established, the end of the century could see a dramatic reduction of tensions along with lower cost security in Europe.

A conventional arrangement of this sort is possible for a number of reasons. First, demographics are working against not only the Soviet Union but also the Federal Republic and most other NATO allies. West Germany will find it difficult to maintain the current size of the Bundeswehr, given the Federal Republic's declining population of young people, while the falling birthrate of Slavic peoples in the Soviet Union—and apprehensions in Moscow about the reliability of non-Slavic troops (particularly those coming from Muslim regions)—creates pressures for cuts in the nearly six million men now fielded by the Red Army. Second, the most effective way for both the West and the Soviets to reduce military costs is to decommission conventional forces. Third, extensive forward positioning of the Red Army is less necessary in an era of increasingly sophisticated and mobile conventional weapons; similar defensive capability can be attained with fewer troops in less aggressive positions.

NATO and Warsaw Pact interests should similarly converge in forging a treaty to ban the use, and force the destruction, of chemical weapons. Both groups should fear the use of such weapons in wars in the Third World, particularly in the Middle East, that could lead to an escalation thereby precipitating superpower involvement.

Underpinning Western Security

NATO—which in May 1988 agreed to study proposals for a "better and more equitable sharing of roles, risks, and responsibilities"—is likely to have reached by the end of the next decade a new modus vivendi for defense cooperation and burden sharing. Assuming a reduction of East-West tensions and asymmetrical conventional force cuts, fewer American divisions will be required on the continent—and therefore one or two of the five U.S. divisions now there could be withdrawn with little risk to western European security or to NATO cohesion. It is also likely that the nuclear deterrent capabilities of Britain and France will be enhanced by that time, a possibility that neither the United States nor western Europe should negotiate away in talks with Moscow. There is likely to be closer nuclear cooperation between Britain and France, as well as expanded coordination between their nuclear force planners and commanders of conventional forces in West Germany. Improvements in intra-European military cooperation will also demonstrate to Americans that Europeans are doing more for themselves. But by the end of the century there still will be no alternative to an American nuclear guarantee and to the presence of some U.S. troops in Europe.

Having passed through a period of austerity-led pressures for unilateral pullbacks from foreign commitments, the United States will have reestablished a domestic consensus in favor of a continued nuclear and conventional commitment to western Europe. And it will have reached a long-term understanding with western Europe to ensure the continued deployment of troops on that continent as long as Soviet forces remain in significant numbers in, or deployed so they could be moved quickly into, eastern Europe.

The question of Germany will raise delicate issues for Washington throughout the 1990s. West Germany is reluctant to modernize short-range nuclear weapons for fear that its territory could become Europe's nuclear battleground. But the United States and other allies are reluctant to allow their nuclear forces in central Europe to become obsolete to the point that they become useless as a deterrent, thus allowing NATO's forward line of defense to be dominated by Warsaw Pact conventional forces. Bonn also wants Washington to negotiate with Moscow to reduce or eliminate those short-range missiles already deployed. West Germans will be increasingly sensitive to what they regard as excessive American intrusion in their daily life—military maneuvers on West German fields, troop transports causing traffic jams on autobahns, and noisy military overflights. These are reminders to West Germans of their nation's dependence on the United States. That dependence takes specific form in West German concern that Washington might interfere in Bonn's efforts to improve ties to East Germany.

Issues relating to growing unease among Germans about their divided status will loom larger and larger in the years ahead. While German reunification is unlikely in this century, it will be revived as a goal by a new generation of West Germans. Movement of people between the two Germanies will be greater and benefits for East Germany (which now enjoys free trade with the EC) will be larger as the Single Market evolves. For the Community, the major goal will be to strengthen its interlocking network of trade and financial ties—leading to greater political and security cohesion—to anchor the Federal Republic firmly to the West, countering any tendency there to seek a Bismarkian "middle ground" in central Europe.

France has proved to be especially cognizant of the need for closer links with Germany, and between Germany and the entire EC membership. Together, these two countries are the driving force for reducing internal barriers in the Community, creating a common monetary system, and forging closer intra-European military ties. Western Europe, having already concluded that great efficiencies are to be gained by reducing internal barriers to non-military trade, has begun to take similar, if more limited steps in the military sector. Recognizing that big additions to defense budgets are unlikely and that cuts are more likely, the western European allies will utilize what is known as the Independent European Programme Group to rationalize weapons research, development, production, and procurement. They will also make advances in sharing maintenance services, cooperate on logistical support and training, and engage to a greater degree in collective weapons contracting.

All of these should enable western Europe to use limited defense funds more effectively. The danger for the United States is that as western European defense cooperation evolves, American firms might find it more difficult to win defense contracts in Europe. A constant debate will ensue over whether America is buying too little of its military equipment from Europe, or Europe is buying too much from America.

A broader political consensus in the West will be required to underpin security relationships. NATO has long had to live with the fact of democracy: when relations with the Soviets improve, citizens of NATO nations become reluctant to support military expenditures and question the need for alliance. NATO governments must see to it that public support for the organization does not depend entirely on the perception of an imminent Soviet threat. The alliance will need to expand the range of issues on which NATO engages the common efforts of the European and North American democracies—from student exchanges, to fighting the drug trade, terrorism, and threats to the environment. All of these will take on greater importance in the 1990s. By moving effectively in at least a few of these areas, NATO can increase its relevance to younger generations, for whom the importance of support for NATO is not as obvious as it is for those whose political views were formed at the height of the cold war.

One particular area in which NATO will need to coordinate more actively is arms control—and Japan will have to be closely involved. Europeans are apprehensive, alternately, when America becomes too belligerent vis-à-vis Moscow and when it appears too compromising. Toughness stirs up apprehensions about nuclear war and gives ammunition to antinuclear groups; active arms reductions talks raise apprehensions over possible decoupling of the U.S. defense commitment from Europe. And if arms cuts are negotiated in Europe and not Asia, the Japanese feel exposed. So America's Atlantic and Asian allies need to be brought into a NATO-centered process of consultations on arms control strategy—which in coming years will involve START, Conventional Forces in Europe (CFE) and perhaps

short-range nuclear forces (SNF) negotiations—both to mini-
mize misunderstandings that breed apprehensions and to ensure that progress on one side of the Euro-Asian landmass does
not add to problems on the other.

Western Europe will often seek to express its views on this
subject in an organized fashion on the basis of a prenegotiated
consensus among European members of NATO—perhaps
forged in the Western European Union or among the foreign
and defense ministers in the European Council, if the EC seeks
to increase its competence in this area.

The United States and the EC will also need an ongoing dialogue to be ready to respond to possible reversals in the Soviet
Union and eastern Europe. As developments in China have
demonstrated, reform is an uncertain process. It could backfire
in many ways in the Soviet Union: if Gorbachev cannot meet
popular expectations for improved living standards, if a blowup
in a Soviet republic threatens stability and is seen by the military as evidence of a deterioration of Moscow's control, if the
communist party believes its authority is threatened by excessive political dissent or a weakening of its control over the economy, or if a blowup in eastern Europe leads to the intervention
of Soviet troops or makes the Soviet Union look impotent by not
doing so. In all these contingencies, Gorbachev could face a
marked decline in his power or be removed. In these circumstances, there is likely to be a backlash that slows or reverses the
process of glasnost and perestroika—or at least retards it significantly—and causes a change in Moscow's more relaxed attitude toward economic and political reform in eastern Europe.
The West will need to factor such contingencies into its economic, foreign, and security policies, even though optimism now
reigns. Division within western Europe, or between it and
America, over how to react to abrupt and adverse change can be
limited by anticipating these possibilities.

Innovations in Consultation

In these and other areas, the United States will need to work not
only with individual western European nations as it has, but
also with the EC—which will likely be the forum for harmoniz-

ing foreign policy among its members on an ever larger range of issues. More frequent discussions between the secretary of state and foreign ministers of a representative group of EC members (perhaps the foreign minister of the nation holding the EC presidency, plus the foreign ministers of the countries proceeding and succeeding in the EC presidency) might be useful—and relations with eastern Europe and the Soviet Union is an apt subject. The Europeans will want these consultations to represent something more than a symbolic act; they will want to be listened to and to feel confident that America gives their views appropriate weight.

If conventional troop negotiations achieve satisfactory results, and economic relations between the EC and its eastern neighbors improve as expected, the United States and its European allies should explore opportunities for convincing the Soviets that their essential security interests will not be compromised, and their economic prospects will be enhanced, by permitting governments to come to power in eastern Europe whose legitimacy is based on genuine voter support, whose survival is not dependent on the Red Army, and which are closely associated with the Community (the second concentric circle around the EC core), although they could remain in COMECON as well. The aim would be for these countries some time in the first quarter of the next century to assume a status similar to that of Finland. A "zone of prosperity and stability" of this sort on the western border of the Soviet Union might become an increasingly comfortable prospect for Moscow in light of expected NATO and Warsaw Pact force reductions, its concern over a possible blowup in eastern Europe under current adverse conditions, and its desire to generate greater prosperity at home (a goal not served by the present economic weakness of its COMECON partners).

As the next decade proceeds, the allies should set in motion a series of consultations with one another to ensure consensus, and then initiate a dialogue with individual eastern European nations, and the Soviet Union, to consider the structure and conditions of such an arrangement. Community leadership of the dialogue with the eastern Europeans and Soviets—consistent with the Paris summit formula on economic help to eastern Europe—would be appropriate. That might provide greater reassurance to the eastern Europeans, and Soviets, than were the United States to appear to dominate the process. It would also alleviate any concerns about a Yalta II agreement made over the heads of the Europeans. The Community should also be one of the guarantors of the integrity of the agreement, although the role of the United States would also be vital in Moscow's eyes.

The role of Japan in Western economic, political, and security strategy will grow over the course of the 1990s as that nation too redefines its global role. Soviet diplomacy will pay increased attention to Asia in the years ahead. Gorbachev has indicated that he intends to cut troop levels in Siberia, and efforts to improve ties with Japan are also to be expected. Given the recent problems in China, Japan's role in Asia—and its importance to the United States—takes on even greater significance. Increasingly, Washington will need to consult Japan on global diplomatic and security issues. NATO as an institution will have to include Japan in its discussions of arms control and East-West strategy, efforts to assist Third World democracies facing economic difficulties, and ways to interdict drug traffic and reverse environmental degradation.

Japan's economic relations with other Pacific Basin nations will intensify over the course of the next decade, perhaps leading to an informal yen zone and to a more institutionalized framework for Asian economic cooperation. But these do not preclude a broader trilateral dialogue among Japan, Europe, and America over a wide range of common interests. Some of these issues are best discussed in the seven-nation economic summits; others will probably be considered in U.S.–EC–Japan talks or in NATO-Japanese discussions.

In the era of John F. Kennedy there was an expectation on both sides of the Atlantic that NATO could become a partnership of equals. This was also a vision of Jean Monnet and Paul Henri Spaak—two fathers of today's Europe. This goal is not likely to be realized by 2000, but a far greater parity is likely. Western Europe will not become a superpower or possess a fully credible nuclear deterrent in this period; nor will it be prepared to exercise a global political role of a scope similar to America's. But it can and will be a powerful global economic force. It will also have forged a more distinct set of European policies and attitudes on global political issues.

The character of the Atlantic relationship will depend heavily on whether America can accommodate western Europe's desire for greater autonomy, a greater leadership role in improving East-West ties, and greater influence on global economic and alliance issues, and on whether western Europe can accomodate America's desire to see Europe assume a greater responsibility for its defense and for global economic stability. If such an accommodation can be reached, the process of normalization between western and eastern Europe can proceed without a weakening of NATO security, and the Community's growing unity will provide the most powerful boost to the fortunes of the West and to democratic values that have been realized in this half of the twentieth century. By the century's end all of Europe will be a safer and more prosperous place.

Military Stability and Political Order in Europe

Johan Jørgen Holst

These reflections concentrate on the relationship between political order and military stability in a period of marked political change. They attempt to trace the roots of some current challenges, as NATO turns 40, and to project their future course. Preventing or deterring aggression has been a primary condition for a stable political order, and that deterrence has been the principal objective of the North Atlantic Treaty Organization (NATO) since its inception.

That task, however, has become much more complex in the age of nuclear weapons, and I examine the existential and operational problems posed by those weapons. The need to restructure and build down nuclear arsenals will become more compelling in the years ahead. Yet those issues cannot be viewed apart from the overall balance of forces, where conventional forces are the major consumer of resources and where asymmetries in that category generate perceived needs for nuclear compensation.

As the situation in Europe becomes more stable, more attention will be devoted to protecting that stability from the turmoil of "out-of-area" conflicts, all the more since NATO members combine global and regional interests in different ways. In such a context, the Atlantic framework will need to be redefined, a task made harder by recurrent debates over abstract, esoteric categories, "decoupling" and "extended deterrence." These reflections must traverse this abstruse landscape.

In a period of rapid change, it is important to preserve both vision and a sense of realism. Hopes become confused with expectations, and both outpace reality. Differences in geopolitical position, historical tradition, and cultural propensities could make it difficult for NATO to fashion coherent coalition policies. It is necessary to keep in mind the geographical asymmetries between the heartland power of the Soviet Union and the island power of the United States, between the continental alliance of the Warsaw Pact and the maritime alliance that is NATO. Under conditions of reduced East-West tension—and, perhaps, few superpower forces deployed forward—the role of naval force will increase.

As the European pillar becomes more visible, with European prosperity and competitiveness having caught up with the United States, how to share the burden of common defense will come to the fore. My reflections thus focus on the many faces of roles, risks, and responsibilities that are carried by the allies. That discussion takes place against the background of rapidly changing East-West relations, offering unprecedented opportunities for reconstruction. Hence, I return to the need to fashion a stable political order. In that connection, the framework for assessing the requirements of military stability is different from that during the period of confrontation.

The Conditions for Political Order

NATO is one of the the most successful alliances in history. Its main success is, of course, that it has prevented war. It has provided a framework for permanent American engagement in the security of Europe, an engagement that has been and remains essential to contain Soviet power. Without that engagement of American island power, Soviet heartland power would pose a clear and present danger of hegemony. Hence, American engagement has constituted an essential condition for maintaining the balance of power.

American engagement was an essential condition for the reconstruction of western Europe after the ravages of the Second World War. It provided the insurance against external aggression and, in turn, permitted the western Europeans to concentrate on their internal reconciliation and to give priority to the reform of their societies, achieving unprecedented levels of welfare and prosperity. This success effectively blunted the ideological challenge of Soviet communism to the democratic order in western Europe, and limited the popular appeal of communist parties in most countries. But, the very success in dismantling Soviet-style communism as a threat to the legitimacy and stability of the democratic order in western Europe tended to increase the saliency of the Soviet military threat. Paradoxically, the success of NATO in defeating the political challenge posed by the Soviet Union thus made the alliance even more necessary in order to cope with the primary threat from Soviet military power.

NATO has provided a framework for addressing the challenge of nuclear weapons in a manner that has prevented their widespread proliferation. Most of the states of western Europe are capable of producing nuclear weapons and could have been moved to exercise the option in the absence of the American nuclear guarantee and participation in the nuclear planning process in the alliance. Nuclear proliferation in Europe would have constituted a major strain on the stability of the security order there and a major stimulant to emulation beyond the continent.

The commitment of most of the western European states to nuclear nonproliferation was a necessary condition for the successful *Ostpolitik* of the Federal Republic and for the general process of rapprochement across the cold war divide in Europe. The alliance has proved to be useful in harmonizing policies toward the East, preventing those policies from becoming a source of tension among the Western nations and an opportunity for Moscow to split those nations.

Preventing Soviet hegemony in Europe is a vital European interest and, equally, a vital American national interest. Should Europe fall under Soviet influence, the global challenge to American security would rise significantly. The legitimacy and continued vitality of the democratic solution would be seriously impaired, affecting choices, expectations, and aspirations everywhere. In the absence of a vibrant western Europe, the United States would become a rather lonely actor on the international scene, gradually succumbing to the introspective and xenophobic perspectives that flow from a sense of being beleaguered.

European and Japanese recovery are monuments to American generosity, to the success of mixed-market economics, and to the productive and innovative capacities of the democratic way. Europe and Japan provide expanded markets for American products, but also competitors to American producers worldwide, including inside the United States. Such competition invariably breeds demands for protectionism, but it also stimulates innovation and increased efficiency.

So, too, European recovery inevitably creates American demands for burden sharing in the alliance and European demands for increased influence on the policies of the alliance. The two themes are related, and their interaction will dominate the politics of the alliance in the years ahead. The question of a redistribution of influence is coming to the fore as East-West relations enter another period of détente. Disagreements between western Europe and the United States concerning the style, content, and priorities of policies toward the East, particularly during the first term of the Reagan administration, have left their imprint on the policy outlooks in European capitals.

For western Europeans, Europe is not only the most important arena in world politics, it is *the* arena. Moreover, European governments are becoming more and more aware of the dangers of being viewed as a playing field for external actors. They want instead to become actors in their own right in order to prevent the European arena from being shaped by the United States and the Soviet Union within the context of their global competition. The importance of this perspective grows as borders in Europe become more porous and "Europe" becomes more real.

The rimland states of western Europe are condemned to share a continent with the Soviet Union. They have no choice but to develop rules of engagement for managing their cohabitation on the continent. They will focus on how to develop cooperative relations that may reduce the saliency of the military confrontation, on confidence-building measures that will protect political relations against disruptions from routine military activity, and on arms control arrangements that will enhance stability by reducing the threat of surprise attack and sustained offensive action. The island power of the United States has *chosen* engagement in the security order of Europe; by implication it retains the option of disengagement. No such option is available to the states of western Europe.

The diversity within the Atlantic alliance is a major source of strength as the world moves beyond the immobility of the cold war. It permits the alliance to deal with peaceful change in a flexible manner. Individual allies can play different roles in regions beyond Europe, providing other nations with a broader spectrum of choice in their international relations than those of a bipolar system dominated by the United States and the Soviet Union. Such diversity of choice may prove particularly stabilizing in Latin America and contribute also to the renaissance of the United Nations that seems to be in the making. On the other hand, this diversity could become a major strain on the unity of the alliance in relation to its primary purposes should it translate into divergent policies vis-à-vis the Soviet Union.

"Crisis" in the alliance has been a recurrent theme in the postwar era, particularly among the pundits who seek to combine the functions of the Oracle at Delphi with the projection of the moral and political conscience of the West. The pronouncements of crisis have failed, however, to become reality. Policymakers have become used to muddling through and to dealing with diversity as a matter of course. Nevertheless, the dual impulses of American unilateralism and European parochialism continue to produce signs of warning on the road ahead. But perhaps the potentially most divisive issue on the horizon is that of the role of nuclear weapons in the defense of western Europe.

The Nuclear Dilemmas

Nuclear weapons are different from other weapons, not only because of the intensity and scale of immediate destruction if they are used, but also because of their long-term impact on human genetics and the physical environment of humankind. The latter effects are well documented but still uncertain in their scale. Nuclear weapons, then, pose moral and existential dilemmas for human beings that are qualitatively different from those associated with traditional warfare. Human beings shy from playing God. Nevertheless, nuclear deterrence has coincided with an unprecedentedly long period of peace in Europe, in spite of intense political rivalry. It would be foolish to deny that this peace was due, at least in part, to the fact of nuclear deterrence.

Nuclear weapons cannot be disinvented. Human beings are condemned to live with the knowledge of how to make them and therefore must be able to arrange the systems of international security so that they are not compelled to use them either by accident or by choice. Even if nations should agree on the total elimination of all existing stocks of nuclear weapons, any future conflict among the major powers will be dominated by the prospect of their reintroduction into the arsenals of war. There is no escape from the nuclear challenge. Nor is there any satisfactory solution.

Nuclear deterrence does not constitute a final solution to the problem of war and peace among nations. Nor does it embody the ultimate expression of human wisdom or compassion. It is no more than a temporary expedient in the continuing search for peace. Nevertheless, it frames some important perspectives.

When Europeans speak of deterrence, they commonly draw a distinction between it and defense. Nuclear weapons are for the prevention of war, not its prosecution. "A nuclear war cannot be won and must never be fought." This simple adage embodies a political perspective that will dominate the public discussion of nuclear issues in the period ahead. Obviously, it simplifies some very complex assessments. The relation between deterrence and defense is no simple dichotomy. Weapons and policies that do not contribute to a capacity for defense could hardly deter. The threat of self-immolation lacks credibility in the world of political calculation. Equally, weapons that could be destroyed in a disarming attack could not provide stable deterrence, since they would draw fire, creating fears of preemption. Reciprocal fears of surprise attack could cause deterrence to break down.

In thinking about the requirements of deterrence, it is worth distinguishing between general and specific deterrence. General deterrence refers to a situation in which neither side considers attacking the other because the prospective costs outweigh the gains, and the risks associated with making the wrong assessment are forbidding. Nuclear weapons are not automatically survivable; they must be made so. Yet the mere existence of large and relatively invulnerable nuclear forces creates a condition of general deterrence (sometimes referred to as existential deterrence). As the major nuclear weapon states have invested heavily in their strategic nuclear forces, general deterrence is considered to be robust rather than delicate. This view, which is likely to gain support in the years ahead, is buttressed by a growing recognition that nuclear weapons create common interests among competing nations that ultimately transcend ephemeral political, economic, and ideological disputes. The common interest in avoiding nuclear catastrophe compels nations to exercise mutual restraint and engage in limited cooperation.

Specific deterrence relates to particular decisions in a crisis. As long as the general political landscape was dominated by competition between East and West, most attention focused on the requirements for specific deterrence, on how to ensure that weapons could survive attempts to disarm them, penetrate to their targets, and be subject to reliable command and control. In the final analysis, deterrence is a state of mind that does not lend itself to precise calculation. It is possible to calculate the probability that weapons will perform in certain ways, but it is not possible to be equally precise about what it takes to deter a given action by a given actor in a given set of circumstances. Political assessment will determine decisions. In a situation of lowered political tension, concerns about requirements for specific deterrence will recede.

Nuclear weapons cast shadows on the political landscape. They affect the expectations and calculations of competitors and bystanders alike. However, the short history of the nuclear era has shown the difficulty of translating nuclear weapons into politically useful currency, of moving beyond nuclear deterrence to nuclear compellence. Nuclear weapons have helped to divorce physical power from political influence. Nuclear power is largely negative power, a power for denial rather than possession, and denial is increasingly confined to a denial of the initiation of nuclear war. Such reasoning applies most particularly to peripheral areas and less to the situation in Europe which is linked so strongly to the central balance of nuclear deterrence between the United States and the Soviet Union. However, if the requirements of deterrence become more salient, so will its limitations.

In the context of a nuclear standoff between the United States and the Soviet Union—a context that is likely to remain an objective fact for the foreseeable future—western European governments came to worry about the political impact of Soviet regional nuclear weapons. Those weapons were viewed as signaling an intention to decouple the western European allies from the nuclear umbrella of the United States, in the shadows of offsetting parity between the superpowers.

Such concerns were at the root of the intense controversy that arose over intermediate-range nuclear missiles in Europe. The primary concern was not the military capacity of the SS-20, for that was of marginal importance. The primary concern was political, a fear lest the Soviet continental-range SS-20 missiles provide the Soviet Union with an option for preferentially threatening the non-nuclear-weapon states in Europe in the event of a crisis. The SS-20 was a challenge to the balance of the political order in Europe, rather than to the balance of military power between the two alliances. The intermediate-range nuclear forces (INF) agreement successfully resolved the issue and established the implicit norm that continental-strike systems should not be allowed to challenge the extended deterrence provided by intercontinental systems.

The INF controversy left another legacy. It demonstrated how the nuclear issue may undermine support for the security policy of democratic states. The reasons are directly related to the special nature of nuclear weapons. All European governments are painfully aware of the disruptive impact of decisions concerning modernization of nuclear forces. But governments in the East are equally aware that stimulating such controversies through nuclear modernizations of their own will create major East-West tensions.

The number of theater nuclear weapons in Europe is very large. It is incommensurate with the concept of nuclear weapons as instruments of deterrence, rather than war fighting, even granting that there is no clear-cut distinction between the two. The large number suggests war fighting, a suggestion amplified by the character of the arsenals, particularly on the Western side, with a heavy emphasis on short-range battlefield forces. As long as the nuclear force posture is the result of military assessments of operational requirements for covering specific target structures, the war-fighting perspective will persist. It will alienate Western societies, eroding support for prudent defense policies. Consequently, the political logic points in the direction of fewer weapons, less reliance on battlefield systems, and withdrawal of nuclear weapons from forward positions (in order to lessen the perception of "use them or lose them" in a crisis).

Restructuring the Posture

If the years ahead see a major breakthrough in the efforts to attain increased stability in the balance of conventional forces in Europe, that breakthrough would alter the nuclear issues as well. If asymmetries in conventional forces were eliminated, the need for nuclear weapons to compensate for such asymmetries would likewise be reduced. The elimination of capacities for short-warning attack would underline the need to restructure NATO's nuclear forces in order to eliminate pressures for early use. Furthermore, many of the categories of conventional weapons that would be first priorities are dual-capable systems—that is, able to deliver both nuclear and conventional warheads. The substantial Soviet advantage in nuclear-capable short-range missiles is an obvious candidate for unilateral or high-priority negotiated reduction.

In fact, a logical concomitant to a regime for conventional stability in Europe would be no first use of nuclear weapons. It would be a de facto rather than a de jure situation; it would be based on the physical and structural character of the postures, rather than declaratory policies, for NATO is likely to eschew formal arrangements that would imply a Soviet *droit de regard* with respect to Western decision making about defense.

A build-down of the military confrontation in Europe would contribute to a further erosion of borders there. At a minimum it would prevent the military competition from solidifying the borders, thus broadening the vista of a more open, pluralistic, and cooperative political order in Europe. American participation in the military aspects of this process will be essential, but European governments are likely to want to take the lead in shaping the political order of Europe in the 1990s—a combination that again will raise complicated questions about roles and responsibilities within the alliance.

Theater nuclear forces presumably contribute to specific deterrence by imposing a need to disperse conventional forces thus limiting their capacity for surprise attack. By threatening retaliation in kind, they constitute a specific deterrent, moreover, to the use of theater nuclear weapons by the adversary. They are thought to contribute to general deterrence by conveying a threat to "lose control," for no one can have high confidence in the ability to limit war beyond the nuclear threshold. Finally, they are meant to contribute to general deterrence by coupling the defense of Europe to the American nuclear umbrella. This function is the most important and also the most conjectural.

The coupling-decoupling debate is another recurrent theme in the history of the Atlantic alliance. The original deployments of theater nuclear forces took place in the context of general American nuclear preponderance and near-monopoly in theater nuclear forces. As the nuclear arsenals grew on both sides, in number as well as in diversity, nuclear deterrence became bilateral at all levels. The old calculus was no longer valid. Europeans, however, continued to view an American commitment to nuclear initiation and escalation as a necessary condition for deterrence; by the same token, American calls for conventional defense and flexible response seemed a way to take American cities off the nuclear hook in Europe, thereby, some feared, making Europe safe for limited war.

During the INF controversy, deployment of cruise and Pershing II ballistic missiles in Europe was thought to enhance deterrence by linking the European battlefield to the American strategic deterrent. It was thought important that the commitment be visible, hence manifested on the ground in Europe. The missiles were to be capable of reaching targets in the Soviet Union and thus of deterring Moscow from contemplating limited war outside its borders in Europe.

However, in the meantime public perceptions had changed. The threat of Soviet invasion, no longer seeming imminent, had been replaced by the threat of nuclear war. Nuclear deployments in Europe were feared by many to betoken a strategy of keeping a war limited to Europe, a vision that could lead the Americans to run greater risks at Europe's expense. Therefore, the logic at the level of national decision making diverged from the perception of large segments of people in society. If Soviet leaders miscalculated the impact of their SS-20 deployments on how European elites saw Soviet intentions, NATO governments miscalculated the impact of their measured response on the apprehensions of their own societies.

Some see the INF treaty as the reward for standing firm and preserving allied unity. Others are more likely to emphasize the negotiating skill and perseverance of Paul Nitze, the "new thinking" of Mikhail Gorbachev, and the priority assigned to restraint by both Moscow and Washington. Nevertheless, most Europeans despair of another modernization debate.

It bears remembering that INF modernization was raised by European governments to the initial reluctance of Washington. Another modernization debate is with NATO as it turns 40, this time involving short-range nuclear forces (SNF). This time in Europe the roles seem reversed, with Washington (and London) the prime mover and most European capitals reluctant. Such reluctance reflects, in part, the legacy of the INF controversy. It also reflects, in part, the changed political environment, expectations of a basic change in the nature of East-West relations in general and the conventional force relation in Europe in particular.

The need for nuclear modernization in order to maintain specific deterrence does not seem persuasive to European publics in such a context, raising the risk of trans-Atlantic estrangement. The problems could be compounded should the impression spread that Europeans are being asked to support the policies of the incumbent American administration against a reluctant American Congress, particularly if a decision in principle should precede decisions on deployment by many years. The political processes will be shaped by impressions that transcend the inherent merits of the particular cases involved.

This suggests a broader issue for the alliance in the years ahead. In the context of détente and arms control, it will prove increasingly difficult to muster public support for prudent defense policies. The issues are more complex than calls for determination and leadership suggest. There is a need to clarify requirements for general deterrence in light of the peacetime management of East-West relations, rather than focusing too sharply on the management of crisis and war, or specific deterrence. Clarifying the limited functions of nuclear weapons in the overall posture will be needed in order to preserve broad social consensus. Decisions based on hard-fought majorities rather than a broadly based consensus would gradually erode support for the alliance.

Real difficulties would arise if American and European views on nuclear weapon requirements came to differ systematically. Imagine, for instance, the recriminations if Europeans ceased to consider American nuclear policies as reassurance but rather viewed them as instruments for taking risks at Europe's expense, or if Americans came to view Europeans as free riders unwilling to shoulder the risks and burdens of the common defense.

The image of American pressure being exerted on Europeans to support controversial defense programs in the American Congress gained currency during the attempts of the Reagan administration to mobilize support in NATO for its Strategic Defense Initiative (SDI) amid widespread public opposition in Europe. It did little to solidify the alliance, much more to contribute to public skepticism. Much as allies should not be allowed to pass the burden of defense on to the shoulders of other allies, they should not attempt to pass the burden of domestic controversy to each other. However, as national security policies generate national controversy, they are likely to involve other allies as well. That is particularly true when controversies arise in the United States, the dominant power within the alliance, but the domestic politics of SNF in the Federal Republic indicate that the spillover is hardly limited to America.

The SNF issue has not been resolved, but the successful NATO summit in 1989, on the alliance's 40th anniversary, paved the way for reasonable management. For the foreseeable future, NATO strategy will require both conventional and nuclear forces in Europe, but the mix will change. A more stable conventional balance at lower levels would require a more stable *theater* nuclear posture as well. NATO has already abandoned some of the systems that seemed to pose pressure for early use, such as atomic mines and nuclear air defenses. Nuclear artillery is the next candidate for being thinned out, or even eliminated, on similar grounds. Systems of short flight time that cannot be recalled, such as SNF missiles, can also be viewed as threats to crisis stability. And, equally important, Europeans will want to be careful not to weaken the INF treaty by extending the range of SNF missiles to the lower limit of that treaty (500 kilometers, or roughly 300 miles).

The SNF modernization decision has been postponed until 1992. The issue will then be examined in a broad political context; by the hopeful timetable set at the 1989 summit, an agreement on conventional force reductions could be nearing implementation and a SNF treaty could be signed. These events would make a completely different context for modernization than that of the late 1980s. An SNF treaty would set the parameters, as yet unclear, but likely to involve smaller numbers and a restructuring away from nuclear artillery toward systems of somewhat longer range. At the same time, programs for restructuring will shape the agenda for the SNF negotiations.

The result might be a small number of SNF missiles (and launchers) with ranges near that of the Soviet SS-21 (120 kilometers or 75 miles), plus nuclear-capable aircraft carrying air-launched missiles of range well below the limits set at the Strategic Arms Reduction Talks (START). Yet by then nuclear restructuring could seem oddly at variance with the process of political reconstruction in Europe: the former would be based on wartime requirements, the latter on the requirements of peaceful change, which could affect the perceived need to keep weapons up to date.

The intricacies of the nuclear calculus should not be divorced from overall political assessments. The danger always exists that expert groups in the alliance will construct a universe of esoteric logical connections forcing ministers to consider menus of specific options rather than basic assumptions. Strategy and force planning become divorced from politics, deriving from narrow abstract constructs rather than overall assessments. In the end, if alliance policies become estranged from the societies of the alliance, those policies will not be sustainable.

The Psychology of Extended Deterrence

The recurrent debate on extended deterrence in NATO has assumed the form of a mystical liturgy. The debate involved struggling with the implications of bilateral nuclear deterrence for the credibility of the American promise to protect western Europe against Soviet aggression. Broadly, political and military perspectives on requirements may be distinguished. In the military perspective, two basic approaches have interacted in the history of the alliance. One involves the buildup of conventional capabilities to contain the Red Army and reduce the claims on the American nuclear deterrent. Its history extends from NSC-68 to the Conventional Defense Improvement program.

The other approach involves attempts to diversify nuclear options so as to increase the likelihood of a nuclear response by making it less apocalyptic. In recent history the diversification of options extends from U.S. Secretary of Defense Robert McNamara's 1962 speech in Ann Arbor through the Schlesinger doctrine (named after his successor, James Schlesinger), to the countervailing strategy of the Carter administration's PD-59, and finally to the Reagan doctrine of prevailing. The counterforce orientation of the approach was designed to introduce more options into the American Single Integrated Operational Plan for nuclear weapons. The approach was never clear-cut in constituting a war-fighting doctrine; rather it begat the notion of assured destruction, which was more of a planning device for sizing the forces than an expression of the requirement for deterrence.

In the political perspective, the preeminent need is to communicate to the Soviet Union that aggression against western Europe would amount to a challenge to vital American interests. The presence of American troops in western Europe lends credibility to this proposition. Extended deterrence in this perspective revolves more around the probability of American engagement in the event of Soviet aggression than around the specific character of the initial response. Deterrence inheres in the uncertainty of the course of events once the threshold of war has been crossed. The political perspective contains the idea that when great powers collide in war there is, as Clausewitz observed, a tendency toward the extremes. Hence, the very presence of American troops in Europe conveys the proverbial threat of "leaving something to chance." Europeans are more likely to embrace the political than the military perspective as the threat continues to recede in the years ahead.

Europeans have tended to be much more relaxed about the size and structure of American strategic forces than Americans have. For the former, windows of vulnerability and marginal asymmetries between the strategic arsenals matter less, simply because first-strike scenarios seem so implausible. Europeans tend toward the pessimistic (or realistic) notion that war does not lend itself to precise calculation, that something will go wrong, that because the uncertainties involved are so large, governments cannot conclude that they could win by striking first. However, that very pessimism also breeds concern about tragic scenarios in which a war breaks out that nobody wants but all fail to avert in a crisis (the 1914 scenario)—a concern that implies a strong NATO interest in a tightly controlled, quite invulnerable American strategic deterrent.

The problem with much of the discussion of extended deterrence is that it tends to focus on logical connections rather than practical issues of the moment, or to deal with the latter in terms of the former. Plainly, any American president would more than hesitate to risk the destruction of New York for the sake of Frankfurt; equally plainly, the United States would prefer to get its cities off the nuclear hook in Europe. Yet U.S. presidents are not confronted with such clear-cut choices. They may be prepared to run some risk to defend Europe against Soviet aggression. Discussions that focus on abstract scenarios of intense crisis or war become divorced from the conduct of peacetime relations, or approach the latter with the former frame of reference.

For instance, from a purely logical position the credibility of the American commitment to defend Europe, if necessary by nuclear retaliation, should increase if the United States were to reduce its vulnerability to Soviet nuclear retaliation. Coming to Europe's assistance then would be less costly to the United States. However, the reactions in Europe to the American Strategic Defense Initiative (SDI) program did not follow this logic. On the contrary, SDI was widely considered to weaken extended deterrence by seeking to make the United States less vulnerable than western Europe to Soviet nuclear destruction. SDI was thought to weaken extended deterrence by heralding an American desire to escape the common condition of nuclear vulnerability.

It was this impulse rather than the outcome that caused concern, because Europeans, generally speaking, did not believe that SDI would work. The United States seemed to want to opt out, pursuing unilateral action rather than accepting interdependence. Through the traditional system of balance of power, Europeans have become reconciled to the predicament of mutual vulnerability. In this sense the arrival of nuclear weapons was more a quantitative change than a qualitative one. Furthermore, Europeans, with their tragic view of history, despaired of a naive American propensity to seek technological fixes to essentially political, even existential, challenges. In addition, governments feared the impact of the exuberant rhetoric promising an escape from the nuclear predicament; the projection of a non-nuclear world, linking the American right with the peace movement on the left in Europe.

The Bush administration is likely to transform the SDI program into a research program to keep pace with the state of the art, moving away from an active pursuit of deployment options. In this manner Washington will increase its freedom of maneuver in the START negotiations and prevent Moscow from stealing the high ground on strategic arms control in Western public opinion.

Toward Enhanced Conventional Stability

American military engagement in western Europe will remain an important condition for the balance of power in Europe. The 325,000 American troops in western Europe provide tangible evidence of the American commitment; they constitute forward defense of the United States and a claim to major influence on the evolution of the political and military order in Europe. However, arms control agreements could lead to a drawdown of that presence, as suggested by President Bush's proposals for the Conventional Forces in Europe (CFE) talks.

The fear of American withdrawal has intruded into alliance politics at critical junctures. Pressure for withdrawal has come from the U.S. Congress rather than any administration in power. Europeans have worried lest a reduction in the American military presence be viewed as an indication of reduced commitment, and so perceptions of security have been associated with specific American force levels, particularly in West

Germany. However, as the sense of danger recedes, the link will loosen.

Moreover, Europeans may come to view explicit or implicit threats of withdrawal as unacceptable dependence. Much as the Mutual and Balanced Force Reduction (MBFR) negotiations with the East in the 1970s were conceived as a way of nailing the Americans to their commitment in Europe, in the 1990s the CFE negotiations may be viewed as a means of stabilizing the American commitment at lower levels and so reducing European vulnerability to threats of unilateral reductions.

NATO, though, is likely to remain the primary framework for the defense of western Europe. A CFE agreement might stimulate European cooperation to maximize the effectiveness of residual force levels, but the perceived absence of danger might weaken political incentives for such cooperation. The Western European Union provides a framework for aligning policy but is far from providing common plans, command and forces. The American lead will continue even in the presence of growing American apprehension about an emerging European pillar. In the final analysis, most European countries prefer American preeminence in the common defense to the preponderance of any single European power or an exclusive grouping of such powers.

It is possible that in the 1990s the American military presence in Europe will be gradually transformed as arrangements for rapid reinforcement replace forward stationing as the principal structure. In other words, the United States may move toward the "Norwegian model," a structure more consonant with the American tradition of the expeditionary forces.

The outlines of an emerging CFE agreement could reduce the danger as major asymmetries—but not all, for some reflect the geopolitical asymmetries of the two alliances—are eliminated. Western studies suggest that reductions must be very substantial in order to improve stability. The Soviet Union is in the process of restructuring its ground forces, moving toward higher tail-to-teeth ratios as well as toward infantry-to-tank ratios.

Under conditions of major reductions, NATO would have to consider similar departures from a linear defense in order to maintain forward defense and the ability to concentrate sufficient forces to protect quickly enough the space that might be threatened. Force-to-space requirements would have to be reexamined, as would the structure of forward defense. The overall strategy of flexible response would not, however, require change to cope with altered conditions. The danger is that flexible response will not be flexible *enough* and will instead be invoked to prevent change in doctrine and force structure. NATO will have to do its homework if it is to retain an up-to-date strategy in a period of deep cuts and restructuring.

Projecting the Atlantic Framework

The Atlantic alliance was the creation of a generation of Americans and Europeans who had shared the experience of defeating German and Italian fascism on the battlefield in Europe. They united in the determination to prevent aggression and dictatorship, a replay of World War II. The successor generations have shared no such traumatic experience. However, they have inherited a pattern of cooperation that has translated into a frame of mind, a point of identification. Europeans worry, nevertheless, about the changing face of America, about the shift of the center of political and economic gravity from the snowbelt of the northeast to the sunbelt of the southwest. The fear is that identification with Europe will weaken as new elites replace the Europe-oriented elites of the eastern seaboard. Some expect the Pacific Basin to replace the Atlantic as the area of major American commitment. Others speculate that social volatility in Latin America may generate the first territorial threats to American security since the Spanish-American War.

However, basic geopolitical interests are likely to keep American security commitments focused on Europe. Soviet power will remain the major global challenge to American interests, and Soviet military power is concentrated in Europe. Containing it there is an efficient way of constraining its worldwide reach. Western Europe, the United States, Canada, New Zealand, and Australia are the repositories of the basic democratic values of Western civilization. If western Europe should come under the sway of Soviet power, a major source of identification for the American way of life would disappear.

The Atlantic alliance is a maritime alliance linking the democracies on both sides of the Atlantic Ocean. It is pitted against a continental alliance dominated by the heartland power of the Eurasian continent sustaining forward deployments in eastern Europe with internal lines of communication. The epicenter of the East-West balance in Europe has been Germany and the central front. Yet the interconnection of the central front and the northern flank has become apparent with the increased capacity of the Soviet Northern Fleet and of Soviet aircraft. If NATO should lose control of the major airfields in Europe, its ability to protect the integrity of the sea lines of communication across the Atlantic would be degraded, along with NATO's ability to resupply the northern flank and the central front. It would thus risk losing a major war, and the balance of political power would tilt in favor of the East.

In a situation of reduced levels of stationed forces on the continent of Europe, the importance of this "law of linkages" would grow as the security of western Europe became more dependent on American reinforcements. Norway will become a more pivotal power in the structure of Western security arrangements. By the same token the relative importance of the U.S. Navy would grow in maintaining the balance of power.

A major issue in relation to the maritime competition in the 1990s will be the scope and role of nuclear sea-launched cruise missiles (SLCMs), in which both the Soviet Union and the United States have active programs. This issue may divide the continental countries of western Europe from Norway. Norway is in a unique position because of its extended coastline bordering on waters in which major naval contests would occur in the event of war. Some of this perspective applies also to the southern flank of NATO, yet the presence of the Soviet Northern Fleet makes Norway's position unique.

From the point of view of the continental powers, SLCMs can be seen as functional alternatives to land-based SNF involving lesser risks of preemptive pressures and societal controversy. Yet from Norway's point of view, SLCMs would redirect the arms race away from deployments on land to the ocean areas off the Norwegian coast. This redirection would project political shadows that would threaten the low tension that has prevailed in the northern areas even during the chilly periods of the cold war. Furthermore, Norway would worry lest American warships with land-attack nuclear SLCMs be withheld from conventional reinforcement of Norway in the event of a crisis for fear of precipitating nuclear escalation.

For the foreseeable future the Soviet Navy is no match for the U.S. Navy in a conventional contest for sea control. Nuclear weapons would change the calculus by becoming an equalizer in favor of the inferior fleet. For NATO the utility of nuclear weapons as force equalizers at sea would appear to be the opposite of what it has been deemed to be on the ground in Europe. Consequently, "conventionalization" of navies, except for dedicated platforms for launching nuclear missiles, may come to be viewed as an attractive option, one to be pursued in arms control during the 1990s.

Naval strategy has not attracted much attention in the alliance at large, but this should change. With fewer American forces *in* Europe, protecting sea lines of communication will become even more important. That means applying the principle of forward defense also to the major threat to those sea lines, the Soviet Northern Fleet. In addition, forward defense at sea is important for direct defense of northern Norway.

However, in the high north naval operations intersect also with strategic operations. Some Americans, including former Secretary of the Navy John Lehman, have suggested using the U.S. Navy to threaten targets on the Kola peninsula in order to dissuade the Soviet Union from pushing its advantage in other areas. Yet this threat of Western horizontal escalation in the high north seems farfetched, because the Soviet Union would appear to enjoy most of the comparative advantages in the region, and because the danger of escalation, of igniting strategic nuclear forces, will seem forbidding. Similarly, strategies for attacking Soviet strategic submarine bastions in the high north would be viewed with apprehension by western Europeans, who would want the Americans instead to concentrate on reinforcing Europe while refraining from operations that increased the danger of escalation. That said, a certain pressure makes sense to compel the Soviet Union to allocate naval combatants to protecting the patrol areas of strategic submarines, thus reducing the forces that might threaten Western sea lines of communication.

Sharing the Burden of Defense

NATO is more than an alliance in the traditional sense. In the 20th century, security policy is no longer the exclusive prerogative of small elites, and cabinet diplomacy is a thing of the past. In democracies, security policy becomes a matter of intense interest, all the more so when nuclear weapons transform it into an existential issue. Nuclear weapons therefore have changed not only the conduct of international relations, but also the relations between state and society in democracies. Politics in NATO thus reflect domestic trends as well as national interests in the traditional sense. Minority and coalition governments increase the leverage of well-organized opinion.

The alliance is in the process of adjusting to changes in the balance of economic power within the Atlantic community as well as beyond it. The American public expects the Europeans to share more of the burden of common defense, while Europeans expect America to share more influence over common policy with regard to the East. At the same time, there is no alternative to American leadership in the foreseeable future, and leadership is related to contribution.

Burden sharing will remain on the agenda. It has many faces. It involves relations between the countries in North America and western Europe, between small powers and the great powers in the alliance, between the countries on the flanks and those in the center of Europe, between the nuclear-weapon states and the non-nuclear-weapon states in the alliance, between the alliance's highly industrialized states and its developing ones. Measuring burdens and benefits is complex, for the burdens involve not only the money that allies contribute to the common defense but also the people, space, and special services. Some contributions lend themselves to easy quantification, while others do not; they are hardly commensurable across the spectrum.

The burden sharing reports of the alliance refer to shared roles, risks, and responsibilities. They recognize that the contributions of allies must be viewed in a broad context and from the perspective of their different visions of their roles in the world. Some allies are able to contribute to international stability by projecting military force, while others focus on contributing to United Nations peacekeeping and official development assistance.

It is necessary to consider defense expenditure broadly, including, for instance, the different opportunity costs of national conscription and professional recruitment. It is critical to focus on outputs, not inputs, to measure and encourage efficiency in the use of defense resources that all the allies will find in short supply.

Yet the problem remains that the popular perceptions may differ from the bargained agreement of alliance managers. Europeans are indebted to their North American allies for making it possible to maintain their security without jeopardizing their prosperity. They should recognize that the American engagement is sustainable in the American domestic political context only if Europeans are viewed as carrying an equitable part of the common burden. The alliance will falter if the view should spread that Europeans are achieving security at the expense of American prosperity. The issues involved are psychological much more than factual, and so it is essential to be careful in conveying the message. Visible demonstrations of common efforts speak more eloquently than statistics, which always retain an image of abstraction and even of special pleading.

Managing East-West Relations in a Period of Rapid Change

The major challenge confronting the Atlantic alliance as it moves into its fifth decade is how to deal with changes in the Soviet Union and eastern Europe. The alliance can cope with discord over policy toward the Third World areas; it cannot continue to function effectively in the event of basic disagreements concerning policies toward the Soviet Union. Differences of emphasis will always exist, but fundamental differences in assessments and objectives would erode the basis for alignment.

In western Europe a broad consensus seems to have emerged around the proposition that Gorbachev's attempt to restructure the Soviet Union be supported, that his success would be in the Western interest. In the United States the issue appears less settled; it is argued that Gorbachev does not intend to bring about basic changes, just some necessary repairs, and that it is not in the interest of the West to assist him or, indeed, for him to succeed. On the contrary, Gorbachev's failure would accelerate the decline of the Soviet Union. The basic orientation to such issues will determine policies on credit, trade, transfer of technology, and arms control.

What constitutes desirable change in the Soviet Union from the point of view of Western interests? By what criteria could the Western allies answer this question? A more efficient Soviet Union could mean a more formidable military challenge, but a more affluent Soviet Union could also imply social demands that would compete with investments in military forces. The relation between the domestic structure and external behavior of states is extremely complex. We should not assume that a more democratic Soviet Union would be more peaceful or that democracy in the Western liberal sense will in fact be tenable there. However, a more open and democratic Soviet Union would be a more reliable partner in arms control.

Gorbachev plainly has decided that in the absence of structural reform the Soviet Union will cease to be a superpower by the turn of the century. He needs finance and managerial expertise to get the country moving again, and he seems convinced that only a certain amount of destabilization will jar a heavily bureaucratized, inefficient, and lethargic system. More conjecturally, he may have become persuaded that military power does not convert directly into politically useful currency; thus the opportunity costs associated with maintaining the large military forces of the Soviet Union are large.

Furthermore, qualitative changes in military technology may confer increasing advantages on the technologically superior competitors—that is, the United States and its allies. Therefore, Gorbachev may have decided to go for arms control as a means of protecting the Soviet position from erosion during a process of military modernization. Finally, his new rhetoric—with its emphasis on social democratic themes of interdependence and mutual restraint—suggests either a basic "new thinking" or a tactical change to elicit positive response in the West.

Uncertainties abound, producing a division in the West between those who see Gorbachev as an invitation to capitalize on competitive strategies in order to defeat the Soviet attempt to remain in the top league and those who see it as an opportunity for the incorporation of the Soviet Union into an international system based on the notions of interdependence and restraint. The Europeans seem to be weighing in overwhelmingly in favor of the latter perspective.

Gorbachev may be defeated by the lethargy of the Soviet system, by a crisis of expectations, or by the dynamics of ethnic conflict in a multinational union. Soviet relations with eastern Europe could turn out to be the Achilles' heel of the waning Soviet imperial order. Gorbachev needs some foreign policy successes in order to retain credibility in his attempts to achieve systemic reforms. As the NATO allies debate how to respond to the Gorbachev phenomenon, they will have to recognize the limits of their influence on the domestic processes in the Soviet Union and to protect themselves against a reversal there. Basically, they should let their approach to the Soviet Union be determined by the standards to which Soviet international behavior conforms.

The successful alliance is entering its fifth decade amid winds of change. Its conduct of East-West relations will be put to the test, primarily in the area of arms control. The arms control process will be concentrated in two fields, strategic arms reduction and conventional stability in Europe. In the former, efforts will be concentrated on completing negotiation of an agreement to cut forces in half. The Bush administration is likely to seek some restructuring of the emerging agreement in order to enhance stability by reducing the warhead-to-launcher ratio, an approach that seems bound to require American concessions on SDI, as the proliferation of offensive warheads would appear to constitute the most cost-effective way of defeating strategic defenses. Such a shift would be welcomed by the European allies of the United States.

The East-West negotiations for conventional stability in all of Europe from the Atlantic to the Urals (and from the Barents Sea to the Mediterranean) will engage the vital interests of all members of the Western alliance. They will require an arduous process in order to establish a comprehensive and verifiable regime of reductions and of security- and confidence-building measures. However, to the extent that Gorbachev requires early successes, a series of unilateral initiatives and limited agreements may seem imperative, making it both more necessary and more difficult to construct a coherent regime of conventional stability. The process could open up numerous possibilities for the Soviet Union to exploit divisions within NATO. It will also underscore Europe's central role in East-West relations and ensure American engagement in its security in the years ahead.

In order to develop concerted perspectives on the challenges and appropriate responses of the 1990s, the alliance would seem well advised to launch another Harmel exercise to shape a framework for its policy, its grand strategy, in the period leading up to the year 2000. The comprehensive concept that was supposed to provide a framework for NATO's policy on security and arms control at the threshold of a new era of negotiations did not suffice. A broader conceptual effort is needed.

The Continuing Threat

Richard Perle

The most formidable challenge facing the NATO alliance now and in the future is to shape the desire of our people for peace and freedom into policies that protect both, and to do so with the confidence of our convictions and the candor to share them. This demands that NATO possess clarity of thought and action, as well as purpose. Above all, it requires that we honor our freedom by providing our people the truth with which to defend it. This is of even greater importance now that we are faced with a Soviet leadership that is pursuing traditional Soviet goals in western Europe with far greater subtlety and sophistication and with a keener eye toward Western public opinion than in the past. Unhappily, however, whatever the virtues of diplomacy in NATO's public discourse, clarity is not among them.

The Need for Clarity

Unlike the Warsaw Pact, the Atlantic alliance has no party line. Its members are free to dissent from majority views and they do so frequently. At the same time they are deeply involved in the shaping of the views that are expressed, in convoluted and often lengthy communiques, at the conclusion of each NATO ministerial meeting. Often these communiqués are the product of a sleepless night during which the bureaucrats of fifteen or sixteen nations have wrestled their English and French languages to the ground in order to paper over differences, avoid controversy, placate public opinion, and round all the corners and smooth all the sharp edges as though they were designing a stealth airplane rather than declaring their most fundamental convictions. No wonder no one reads these official pronouncements except those who draft them and, from time to time, an opposition party looking for a quarrel with its own government.

For too long NATO's ministers have sacrificed clarity to consensus. And then we wonder why the public is confused about defense and security issues and even, if some European polls are to be believed, about whether the president of the United States or the general secretary of the communist party of the Soviet Union is the more sincere in the pursuit of peace and arms control.

How can we possibly be convincing when we cower behind bland and oblique formulations so as not to offend the sensitivities of our enemies or the prevailing wisdom of our editorial writers? Add to the *sotto voce* murmurings that pass for alliance statements the tendency to embrace every fashionable idea, no matter how ill founded, and you have a recipe for diplomatic drift and political disaster. It is pointless to complain about the inroads of Soviet propaganda while joining in the charade that permits it to succeed. There is, in all of this, an unconsciously patronizing quality to the way we choose—both as an alliance and, often, as leaders of member governments—to communicate with our people. It is wrong to believe that they must be protected, by officials wiser than themselves, from knowledge of the source and nature of the danger that threatens our security and democratic institutions. They possess the strength and resilience to face unpleasant truths if these are only laid before them.

On such complex subjects as military strategy, defense spending, chemical weapons, nuclear testing, arms control, Soviet treaty violations, or international terrorism, a failure of forthrightness or just plain silence—particularly among the European members of the alliance—often has led to confusion and wishful thinking of alarming proportions. In such a climate reality is subordinated to hope, and policy is shaped by fear.

Consider the notion that an agreement to abolish all nuclear weapons would enhance our security and diminish the threat of a nuclear war. This idea was artfully and disingenuously cultivated by General Secretary Gorbachev in his January 1986 proposal to eliminate all nuclear weapons by the year 2000. It is dangerous nonsense, calculated to undermine the legitimacy of weapons that are vital to Western security—and to whose numbers the Soviets have been adding steadily for the past two decades.

For a quarter-century NATO has relied on nuclear weapons to offset a massive Soviet superiority of conventional forces—a superiority that will remain even if the Soviets carry through on their proposal to reduce their forces stationed in eastern Europe. And even as Soviet theater nuclear forces have grown to exceed those of the Western allies, we have sought to confront the Warsaw Pact with the threat of escalation, however unlikely, to deter aggression. Exhortations to diminish dependence on nuclear weapons by strengthening conventional defenses have been unavailing. And despite the abhorrence of nuclear weapons routinely expressed by those least prepared to pay for conventional ones, the alliance remains unwilling to invest in a more favorable conventional balance with the Warsaw Pact.

To talk, in these circumstances, of the abandonment of nuclear weapons and the substitution of a conventional deterrent is absurd. Indeed, the very concept of deterring the Soviet Union with conventional weapons—however much they might be improved, however many divisions NATO might raise and equip—is hopelessly unrealistic. For while conventional *defense* is both possible and desirable (and expensive), conventional *deterrence* is a dangerous illusion. Even if NATO mounted a superior conventional force, it could not deter the Soviet Union with its vast nuclear arsenal.

And as for the Soviet's agreeing to eliminate nuclear weapons, what Western leader would turn in his country's last remaining nuclear weapon on the strength of assurances—mere words—that the Soviets had done the same? The simple truth is that the verification of an agreement to abolish all nuclear weapons is not difficult, or very difficult: it is *impossible*, and Mikhail Gorbachev knows it. Indeed, he counts on it. It enables him to propose eliminating all nuclear weapons with full confidence that the West cannot agree. And he has the added insurance that if we were so foolish as to do so, the Soviet Union, which would surely cheat, would wind up with a monopoly of nuclear weapons and the realization of the Leninist dream of a decisive correlation of forces. For this reason alone it is idle to speak of conventional deterrence or a nuclear-free world.

The foolishness of a nuclear-free world is in no way mitigated by the "conditions" that Western statesmen routinely attach to its achievement in order to avoid dismissing the idea as the empty propaganda that it is. It is self-defeating obfuscation to argue that eliminating all nuclear weapons is a good idea but the year 2000 is too soon, or to suggest that the process must advance by steps or stages, or that it must await a more favorable conventional balance or the settlement of regional disputes. These arguments—rationalizations, really—are deployed by officials and politicians who fear that the public would not support them if they simply rejected outright Mr. Gorbachev's beguiling maneuver.

This is a profound mistake. Our people are more realistic than many politicians and most foreign offices think. They will work their way through an issue like this one, and they will understand it clearly. But they will understand it sooner and with greater confidence if their leaders earn their pay and begin to lead. There is a reason why French public opinion has been consistently more realistic about these matters than opinion elsewhere in Europe and it surely lies in the greater candor of a succession of French leaders, and a sometimes admirable French capacity to hold fast in the face of pressure from outside.

The Soviet Union's call for an end to all nuclear testing and the moratorium with which it has sought to pressure the United States along these lines present similar issues for the alliance. As long as the United States depends on nuclear weapons for its own defense, and that of its allies, the testing of nuclear weapons will be necessary. Without testing we would lose confidence in the weapons in our inventory; we would lose the capacity to correct failures and validate the corrections; and we would bring to a halt a critical element in the process by which we have been reducing the number and yield of nuclear weapons while making the residual stockpile safer, more secure, and more survivable.

The conduct of nuclear tests over the last quarter-century has been vital to the development of weapons that are, in turn, vital to the credibility and effectiveness of the American nuclear deterrent and NATO strategy. The idea that it would be a good thing to halt the testing of nuclear weapons is based on the beliefs that the development of new nuclear weapons is a bad thing and that the inevitable decline in confidence in weapons that cannot be tested would somehow make their use less likely. Neither belief holds up under analysis.

The development of new nuclear weapons—most often as a replacement for older weapons that are less reliable, less safe, and less effective—has made deterrence more robust and the nuclear threshold higher than it would have been. The leadership of the alliance has known all of this for some time. Nevertheless, a number of allied leaders have urged the United States to abandon nuclear testing, or restrict it sharply. And a number of American officials, who are persuaded of the need to test nuclear weapons, have sought over the years to avoid saying so by declaring an end to testing a "long-term goal" and by pointing to the inability to verify a comprehensive test ban as the central argument against it. The Reagan administration was the first to express in public a view that previous administrations had held in private: that a comprehensive test ban would be dangerous and undesirable even if it were verifiable—which it is not.

Thus the West, by hiding behind verification, and by its silence in public about the necessity to test, has helped to set the stage for Gorbachev's moratorium. And by declaring that a comprehensive test ban is a long-term goal, we have obscured the necessity for, and the benefits of, nuclear testing. Those who know better have joined with those who do not.

In this intellectual climate the Kremlin has found it easy to make us an offer that we must refuse; we, in turn, have made that refusal more costly and less intelligible than is warranted or wise.

tions. The radar at Krasnoyarsk, the deployment of a second new type of inter-continental ballistic missile (ICBM), the encryption of telemetry necessary to establish compliance, to name but a few, are all well known.

NATO has, from time to time, had something to say on the subject, and various alliance leaders have found occasion to comment as spokesmen for their governments. Yet in all the pronouncements I cannot recall seeing the word "violation." There have been "concerns" and even "serious concerns" expressed about the Soviet record of compliance. There have been appeals pointing to the importance of compliance and warnings about a double standard of compliance; but nowhere have I been able to find a statement deploring and denouncing cheating by the Soviet Union. It is as though the words "violation" and "cheating" cannot be spoken in well-mannered company. How hard our allies find it to distinguish between the unspeakable and the unspoken. How easy it is to become like parents who, wishing to avoid the pain and inconvenience of disciplining their children, will pretend not to have noticed their misdeeds.

In response to Soviet violations, President Reagan felt it necessary to decide that the United States would no longer consider itself bound to comply with the provisions of the first Strategic Arms Limitation Treaty (SALT I) interim agreement and the unratified SALT II Treaty. His misgivings about SALT II, which the Senate Armed Services Committee shared in 1979 (when it found that ratification of the treaty was not in the national security interests of the United States), were well known. Nevertheless, the president's action was taken reluctantly, and only after repeated and unsuccessful attempts to persuade the Soviets to end their violations and comply with the agreement. The decision also followed more than five years of compliance by the administration, which early in 1981 had pledged to refrain from any action that would undercut SALT II so long as the Soviets demonstrated similar restraint.

In contrast to the halting euphemisms with which American allies questioned Soviet compliance with SALT II, their desire that the United States continue unilaterally to comply found clear expression at ministerial meetings and in many bilateral consultations. Allied governments found it easier to distance themselves from the American response to Soviet violations than from the violations themselves. The double standard, condemned in NATO communiqués, was urged upon the United States. And because so little was said about Soviet cheating, the American response to it was made to appear capricious and unfounded. The price of silence in 1983 became incomprehension in 1986. The lesson in all these instances is as clear as it is unlearned: if we fail to frame the debate within which the NATO alliance considers issues of security and arms control, if we shade reality in the belief that its glare is too harsh for our people to comprehend, we will leave it to be shaped by our adversaries for their purposes and in their image.

The State of the Alliance

With the single exception of Prime Minister Margaret Thatcher in Britain, the 1980s did not see a strong leader among America's European allies. West German Chancellor Helmut Kohl, who rose to a position of strength just before the deployment of medium-range missiles late in 1983, has never equaled it before or after. Forced into a coalition with the Free Democratic Party (FDP), Kohl all but ceded authority over security policy to Foreign Minister Hans Dietrich Genscher.

In France a desire for strength and independence was qualified by budget pressure and the inefficiencies of nonintegration into the NATO military structure. In Belgium and the Netherlands a strong attachment to NATO continued, but the government of neither could be expected to take assertive positions (especially on nuclear matters) or lead the alliance. Luxembourg and Iceland, faithful but small, were more a moral encouragement than anything else. Italy was steady and reliable, but its defense investment has declined and is likely to decline further.

To the north, the Danish government was forced to obtain support from its socialist opposition on major security issues, including the size of the steadily shrinking budget. Norway has done little to strengthen the alliance in recent years despite the excellence of its military leadership, and at times it encumbered exercises and forward planning in order to accommodate anti-military opinion.

To the south, NATO was hardly strengthened by the admission of socialist Spain, whose first significant act, after refusing to join the NATO integrated military structure, was to force the removal of the American 401st Tactical Fighter Wing from Spanish territory without even a pretense of compensating for this lost capability. Portugal, a faithful ally, did what it could within the limits of its resources.

In the southeast, NATO was weakened by the attitude of Greek Prime Minister Papandreou, who could not seem to decide whether Turkey or the United States is the greater villain. The quarrel between Greece and Turkey plagued the alliance on its vital southeastern flank, disrupting important exercises and impairing necessary planning and infrastructure development.

In North America, the Canadian contribution to NATO declined steadily; it is now among the lowest in the alliance. And while the United States spent generously in the first Reagan term to rebuild American defenses, the years since then have seen a decline, with the prospect of further decline to come.

In the present climate of improving superpower relations, the successful conclusion of the intermediate-range nuclear forces (INF) treaty, and the impending conventional arms control initiatives, NATO countries are reexamining their military strategies, force postures, and defense expenditures. Inevitably, with this reassessment the issue of burden sharing will once again be in the forefront of alliance politics. The disproportionate share of the burden of defending the NATO alliance shouldered by the United States was a source of considerable friction throughout the 1980s and promises to continue in the 1990s. While I believe it is wise for the United States to defend our interests as far forward as possible, our defense effort, from which our allies also derive protection, could be shared, and should be shared, more equitably.

Sharing the Burden

Of course, one must define the burden to be shared in order to judge whether it is being shared fairly. For the most part our allies' commitment to the common defense is limited to countering immediate threats to their security and territorial integrity. Thus they do not consider that they are under any obligation to join the United States in the protection of Western interests outside their immediate territory. When these interests are threatened elsewhere—for example, in the Persian Gulf—individual allies may or may not join with us, depending on decisions made individually and at the time. But in no case do they consider that the NATO alliance obliges them to do more than protect NATO territory. For this reason the burden of protecting Western interests falls even more disproportionately on the United States than the figures might otherwise suggest.

I have listened on many occasions to a recitation of statistics showing that the European NATO allies provide a high percentage of the men and equipment that are deployed in defense of the alliance. Without these troops, ships, and aircraft, an already adverse NATO/Warsaw Pact conventional force balance would be even more lopsided than it is now. But that fact in no way relieves the allies of the responsibility for making a defense effort more nearly comparable to that of the United States. Indeed, to say that America benefits from the effort of its allies, and they from ours, is merely to underline the collective nature of our alliance.

The best known—and most telling—input measure used to calculate burden sharing is the percentage of gross domestic product (GDP) member countries devote to defense spending. In 1987 the United States invested 6.5 percent of its GDP in defense. The figure for the Federal Republic was less than half, 3.1 percent. Canadian investment amounted to 2.1 percent, less than one-third the proportion the United States was spending.[1] And Japan, despite its large and growing wealth, spent barely 1 percent, a scant one-sixth of the U.S. budget.

The American budget deficit is not caused by defense expenditure, and it is galling to be lectured, as Americans so frequently are, by those they defend about the need to control the budget deficit. Indeed, if the United States were to reduce its defense effort to say, the level of the Federal Republic (expressed as a percentage of GDP), it could balance the 1989 budget. Such a move would gravely imperil American security, as well as the security of Germany, and no one concerned about security would recommend such a course. But it does help to place in perspective the mounting frustration with which many Americans view the superfluity of advice fired in our direction by finance ministers who have reduced the defense ministers of Europe to hapless supplicants.

The disparity in the division of the financial burden is plainly evident, even though no single set of figures adequately express the various ways in which NATO allies contribute to the common security. A report of the NATO Defense Planning Committee in December 1988, while calling for objective and accepted burden-sharing indicators, emphasized the complexity of the issue and cited quantifiable and nonquantifiable contributions. The report noted that sacrifices made by European nations in making available people and space or accepting limitations in personal freedom or the quality of life are by no means trivial elements of the burden. Certainly this is true, but in arguing that the United States assumes an unfair share of the defense burden, I have in mind more than quantifiable financial and technical resources. As inadequate as the performance of the allies is with respect to defense spending, the most glaring inequities lie elsewhere.

First, not only does the United States make a larger contribution by protecting Western interests throughout the world, it also assumes greater risks in the defense of its allies than they are prepared to assume in America's defense or, in some cases, their own. No American ally has been prepared to take anything approaching the risk the United States assumes in its commitment to use nuclear weapons to defend other countries. (This may help explain why there are doubts as to the credibility of that commitment.) Some NATO allies do share the nuclear risks by having American nuclear weapons deployed on their territory. But others—Denmark, Norway, Spain, Iceland, Luxembourg, Portugal, and Canada—refuse to accommodate nuclear weapons on their soil. And there is pressure in West Germany, which now accepts American nuclear weapons, and among such opposition parties as the British Labour party, to remove all nuclear weapons. Not even France and Britain, which maintain independent nuclear deterrent forces, have been prepared to extend a nuclear guarantee to other members of the alliance.

Second, consider the American policy of providing security assistance to the less-developed NATO members. While the United States does not do nearly enough to support such countries as Portugal and Turkey, the wealthier allies do practically nothing. It is not as if they cannot afford to extend aid. Britain, France, West Germany, Denmark, Norway, Italy, and the Netherlands—and, outside NATO, Japan—could all lend greater assistance to Turkey, which urgently needs to equip its sizable army with modern military equipment.[2] In any alliance in which all burdens were shared fairly there would be a significant flow of aid from the better to the less well-off members. However, with respect to NATO, this simply has not been the case. In 1986 the United States provided $1 billion in military credits and aid, while West Germany contributed DM 300 million.[3] Assistance from all other member countries has been, at best, minimal.

Third, there is the matter of restraint in supplying advanced technologies and know-how to the Eastern bloc. Most of our allies would cheerfully sell the Soviet bloc those advanced technologies that would enable the Soviets to strengthen greatly the effectiveness of their military forces. Indeed, many do so—or they at least countenance such transactions by companies under their jurisdiction by failing to put in place even a minimally effective system of export controls. Recently, when Japanese and Norwegian firms sold the Soviet Union the means by which to counter anti-submarine warfare capabilities, the damage was enormous. The long list of such examples encompasses optical, radar, deep-submersible, advanced materials, microelectronic, manufacturing and scientific technologies. At the Coordinating Committee (COCOM) in Paris, which is charged with coordinating restrictions on the sale of sensitive technology to the Warsaw Pact nations, the European allies are an unrelenting source of pressure to relax restrictions and to increase the flow of these goods. The West Germans in particular have shown a remarkable indifference to the military consequences of some sensitive sales to the Soviet Union, and they seem eager to do even more in the future.

Fourth, consider the nature of the financial relationship between many of our allies and the Soviet bloc. Western commercial banks have been lending money to the Soviet Union in prodigious amounts. In 1986, the average monthly lending by European and Japanese banks to the Soviet bloc was $2 billion, of which $1.6 billion took the form of untied, general-purpose loans available to the Soviets to finance their military buildup and their subversion abroad. Japan has recently emerged as the largest single source of Soviet bloc credits—accounting for 40 percent, while 30 percent from the West Germany.

The Germans, who cannot get their defense budget up to half of the U.S. share of GDP, are eager to further expand their financial relationship with the Soviets with an inevitable expansion of untied lending. In 1988 the European allies tripped over each other in a rush to lend Moscow money. The lending frenzy netted Moscow a $1.6 billion line of credit from West German banks, ostensibly to help modernize the Soviet's food and consumer goods industries, and Italy granted $775 million in trade credits. The Italian trade credit reportedly was even extended on a subsidized, low-interest basis, which would be in violation of allied agreements against subsidized loans.

Fifth, there is the problem of what one might call reciprocal sensitivity to the security concerns of other allies. The allies expect the United States to share the burden of protecting their interests when they consider that those interests are in jeopardy. Over the years, the United States has provided logistical support to a number of allies whose overseas interests were threatened—France, Belgium, and Britain for instance. And where are they when America needs help—for example, in containing Cuban or Nicaraguan subversion? If they are to be found at all it is often on the side of U.S. adversaries. The European Economic Community (EEC) collectively and a number of its members individually cannot manage to find meaningful funds for such allies as Turkey, but they have managed to send aid to the Sandinistas. They have, as well, largely scorned the effort to contain Castro by limiting trade and financial transactions with his regime.

I do not wish to overstate the point; the record here is mixed. But it is intolerable that allies of the United States, who have seldom found the resources to assist other allies, should actually send aid to our adversaries. Obviously, on such issues as Cuba and Nicaragua there is room for allies to disagree. But in any cohesive alliance there should be a willingness to defer, whenever possible, to the views of the ally most immediately concerned.

Sixth, take the issue of access and overflight rights for American forces and base facilities for U.S. overseas deployments. As the fine report of the Commission on Integrated Long-Term Strategy, chaired by Fred Iklé and Albert Wohlstetter, pointed out, the reluctance of allies to facilitate the movement of American forces could pose critical problems in projecting power in support of objectives that are largely shared, at least privately, by many of those allies. France's refusal to permit overflight of its territory for American forces engaged against Libya is a case in point. And, as the expulsion of the 401st Tactical Fighter Wing from Spain makes clear, some allies are not prepared to accommodate even those minimal facilities necessary for the conventional defense of the alliance. Even where the United States is able to secure base facilities, the negotiations of the necessary agreements are becoming rather more like real estate transactions than collaborative efforts among allies.

What should be done to bring about a more equitable sharing of the burdens of Western security? The arguments suggests the answer:

• The European economy, like the Japanese, is flourishing. West Germany, Italy, the United Kingdom, France, Denmark, Norway, and the Netherlands could all do more to invest in defense, especially in conventional forces, without affecting the well-being of their economies or sacrificing social programs.

The American policy of leading by example in the early years of the Reagan administration, when the United States greatly increased defense spending, has failed. Now that the United States is reducing its own defense investment, it hardly commends a policy of "follow America." Aside from greater direct investment in defense, increased assistance to Turkey and Portugal in Europe and the Philippines and others elsewhere is well within the means of the major allies.

• The allies cannot assume, but they can surely share more effectively, the risk associated with NATO's policy of deterring aggression through nuclear threats. They can and should publicly support the plan agreed to at Montebello in 1983 to modernize the nuclear weapons that will remain in Europe after all intermediate-range missiles have been withdrawn. They can also improve their conventional forces so as to diminish the extent to which we rely on the threat to use nuclear weapons in response to aggression carried out by conventional means.

• Actions that actually add to NATO's defense burden, like the sale of sensitive advanced technologies and the extension of untied loans, could be halted or at least curtailed. The allies should act to strengthen the controls on the export of sensitive technology to the Soviet bloc, and they should take steps to enforce those controls.

• It is also well within the capacity of our allies to permit American forces greater access to the bases and facilities on their territory—and to do so in a manner that gives confidence enough to plan, that they will be there when the United States needs them.

Defining the Threat

One possible explanation for European reluctance to increase defense spending lies in their perception of the threat. I have seen enough of the European leadership to believe that many prime ministers, ministers of foreign affairs, finance ministers, and other political leaders are woefully ignorant of the nature of the military balance between East and West. Compared with their American counterparts they are poorly informed; many have never had a comprehensive briefing on the status of the NATO and Warsaw Pact military forces of the sort that is routinely made available to members of the American Congress. I cannot recall the last time that a NATO foreign ministers' meeting was briefed in depth on these military matters. And while NATO defense ministers regularly receive such briefings, they often lack influence within their own governments. At meetings of NATO defense ministers one invariably hears a plaintive lament to the effect that things would be different if only more people could see the evidence that has been laid before them. No doubt the defense ministers have their chancellors, presidents, foreign ministers, and finance ministers in mind.

The point of all this is to disagree most emphatically with those who draw one of two wrong conclusions from the apparent indifference of some allied officials toward the Soviet military threat to Europe. One conclusion is that it is we Americans whose perception is impaired, with the result that we exaggerate the weight of Soviet military forces. Another is usually formulated like this: If the Europeans, who are closer to the Soviet Union than we are, don't seem concerned with the Soviet threat, why should America be so troubled? In both cases the answer is that if allied officials had the same access as their American colleagues to the steady stream of intelligence pointing to the unrelenting buildup of Soviet military power, they would react much as Americans have—with concern and apprehension and even money. So it remains an important task of American diplomacy—which to date has largely failed—to get the facts before the community of allied officials, whose knowledge and judgment are crucial to the development of sound policies. This will be even more critical in the 1990s, given Mikhail Gorbachev's proposal to unilaterally withdraw large numbers of Soviet troops and tanks from eastern Europe. While surely significant politically, and marginally so from a military point of view, the United States must remind its allies that Warsaw Pact forces will still maintain military superiority over NATO.

For all that is changing, and will change by the year 2000, one imperative has not changed and will not do so—that of counterbalancing Soviet military power in Europe. The United States cannot coerce its allies, but it should not shrink from reminding them of that fact. For 40 years NATO has survived the most calculated actions of its adversaries. Whether it will survive the least calculated actions of its members remains to be seen.

Notes

1. NATO Press Service, "Financial Data Relating to NATO Defense," Press Release M-DPC-2(88) 74, December 1, 1988.
2. The Federal Republic has made available substantial foreign aid to Turkey in recent years.
3. NATO Defense Planning Committee Report, *Enhancing Alliance Collective Security: Shared Roles, Risks and Responsibilities in the Alliance* (Brussels, December 1988.)

The Challenge of Gorbachev

David Owen

The major challenge facing Europe and America is how to respond to the new face that the Soviet Union presents to the world, a face personified by President Mikhail Gorbachev. In 1988 we saw the end of the cold war. It had lasted since the blockade of Berlin, a relentless period of four decades in which Stalin's legacy continued long after his death. Yet in 1989, we certainly do not see an end to the ideological war, even though too many people are pretending that we do. Soviet communism is changing fast and will continue to change, but the party is not going to give up the reins of power, even though the horsemen are very different. Nor will Soviet communism easily lose its appetite for worldwide power.

The best way for the West to respond is by addressing those problems that are causing anxiety within the democratic groupings. Whether it be done in the North Atlantic Treaty Organization (NATO) or the Western European Union (WEU), or in the Organization for Economic Cooperation and Development (OECD) or the European Community, there are problems to be faced and solved. Only when the West has secured agreement within its own organizations on the issues that divide it will it be able to forge an effective consensus on the best approach to the Soviet Union.

In this context, the debate over short-range nuclear forces (SNF), in which the Federal Republic openly differed with the United States and Britain over modernization of the Lance missile, had one advantage: the Western nations were no longer able to avoid serious internal debate within NATO on how to react to the Soviet Union. Instead of continuing to deal with vital questions involving the Soviet Union on an ad hoc basis, the West had to recognize that there are different perceptions within NATO and had to grapple with those differences. No longer can we respond case by case. For the more we respond in a uncoordinated way to the flurry of Soviet initiatives, the easier it will be for the Soviet Union to secure its objectives without meeting any of ours. And the harder it will be for us to achieve unity among ourselves, for the potential exists for two fissures in a united Western front, that between western Europe and the United States, and that between the two Germanies. The Soviet Union has never ceased to probe those cracks and to do what it can to lever them apart.

Historical Reminders

At the start of any honest reappraisal of East-West policy, it is no bad thing to remind ourselves of some salient historical facts. Western Europe's interests have not always been, nor will they always be, totally the same as those of the United States. Not surprisingly, American presidents have pursued policy objectives during this century with less regard for western Europe's interests than Europeans might have liked. The United States did not deploy troops on the ground of continental Europe in support of France and Britain until the spring of 1918. Nor did President Roosevelt feel able to come into World War II while Britain was standing virtually alone in Europe in 1940; he waited, instead, until after Japan had attacked the U.S. fleet in Pearl Harbor in 1941.

At Yalta, Roosevelt had a somewhat starry-eyed view of Stalin's intentions. While President Truman was far more realistic than Roosevelt, he still agreed to cut off all wartime nuclear collaboration with Britain in 1945, when Congress passed the infamous McMahon Act. In 1956, under President Eisenhower, the United States put pressure on the pound sterling to force Britain and France to pull back from occupying the whole of the Suez Canal when both were cooperating clandestinely with Israel. In 1978, President Carter came very close to making an explicit no-first-use-of-nuclear-weapons statement, but was dissuaded by British Prime Minister James Callaghan. In 1986, President Reagan at Reykjavik was ready to contemplate scrapping all ballistic missiles without consulting his European allies, even his close friend, Prime Minister Margaret Thatcher.

Soviet-European relationships are also worth a historical look. Fifty years ago, Britain was an enemy of the Soviet Union, two years later the two were allies, and five years after that, cold warriors. The Nazi-Soviet Pact of August 1939 is now being presented in the Soviet Union as a foolish act by Stalin, allowing the Germans to first occupy France and then mount a one-front Russian campaign. However, Stalin knew how vulnerable his country was, not just militarily, but as a result of his purges. It will be very revealing if the next Soviet skeleton to be disinterred is the number of Russians who joined arms with the invading Germans.

Who can be sure today that the Soviet Union will not reverse its postwar hostility to the rebirth of a unified Germany and become its midwife? What the Soviets are doing is creating a climate designed to tempt the West Germans to pour money and technology into the modernization of the Soviet economy. If the price is further relaxation between East and West Germany, even to the point of unification, who can be certain that the traditional fears of France, Britain, and the United States will not come true and a Soviet-German alliance be reestablished? This time, in contrast to 50 years ago, the Soviet motivation would be an economic one. If the Soviets fear revived German militarism, they might insist that neutralism is the price of reunification.

How the allies respond to the issues surrounding reunification will bear heavily on public opinion inside Germany. Reunification is always on the agenda, if not as an immediate or even a medium-term issue. The West could, however, force it to the top of the political agenda by appearing to oppose reunification, thus seeming to pass a no-confidence vote on West German democracy. We should trust enough in the robustness of postwar West German democracy to encourage West and East Germany to reunify, but within the Western democratic grouping of nations. If the East Germans want one country, let them accept a vote of all its citizens. It is likely that such a vote would favor not just membership of the European Community, but also membership of the Western European Union and even NATO. If the United States, Britain, and France reject reunification, they will confirm the case for those Germans who already believe that the only route to reunification is through neutralism.

The Need for Nuclear Modernization

A central principle of NATO's nuclear deterrence is that it is the political responsibility of all members. As far as possible, NATO should avoid developing two classes of members, those who accept nuclear weapons on their territory and those who do not. Some NATO members are nuclear-weapon states, and others are not, yet it has been important that Spain, Norway, Denmark, Holland, Italy, Greece, and Turkey have all in various ways accepted that ships from NATO's navies visiting their ports may have on board nuclear weapons. For similar reasons, West Germany and Belgium, non-nuclear-weapon states, have been ready to accept on their territory the U.S. F-111s and F-15Es and British Tornado aircraft. These now carry nuclear bombs but soon will have nuclear-armed standoff air-to-surface missiles. If Franco-German defense cooperation becomes even closer, French nuclear-armed aircraft may eventually be stationed on other European nations' territory as well.

The United States should offer to forge a partnership with France and Britain to develop such standoff nuclear missiles. This would mean moving Britain away from buying purely American hardware. It would also start to link the British and French nuclear deterrents with American stealth technology, and would improve the penetration of the existing French standoff missile, at present of too short range. NATO should be able to agree on this modernization.

Indeed, if Europe is to develop its own defense identity over the long run, it is essential, as long as the Soviet Union has nuclear weapons, for Europeans to own part of the West's nuclear deterrent. This will require coordination between the two western European nuclear states, France and Britain. Since the mid-1970s, the United States has given France, under three different governments, significant covert help in nuclear weapons technology. It is time this covert help was openly acknowledged as a matter of principle. Doing so would send a message to the Soviet Union about the future strategic shape of western European security and put the Lance debate in a better perspective.

For NATO not to modernize some of its nuclear and conventional weaponry during the arms control negotiations that lie ahead would be an act of reckless folly. Replacing the free-fall nuclear bombs on aircraft is an essential Western modernization that must be given political approval. The United States F-111, the French Mirage, and the British Tornado aircraft will be given a new lease on life with a standoff capability, becoming less vulnerable to attack if they do not have to overfly their targets.

By contrast, nuclear artillery has for years been a class of weapons that NATO could safely give up completely. The alliance should do so unilaterally, as a confidence-building measure, without putting it into the East-West negotiating process. Done unilaterally, on the recommendation of the Supreme Allied Commander, Europe (SACEUR), it would also be a good public relations response to Gorbachev's unilateral decision to remove some short-range nuclear missiles.

The quality of American leadership will be crucial in this process of selective modernization. Washington will need to reach a clear understanding with France and Britain on nuclear strategy. France shows a new flexibility; its readiness to participate in the new Conventional Forces in Europe (CFE) talks after staying out of the Mutual and Balanced Force Reduction (MBFR) negotiations, is welcome, and President Mitterrand seems ready to rethink France's short-range Hades missile. In 1988, Mitterrand criticized any successor to Lance—in sharp contrast to Mrs. Thatcher, who wanted to modernize the full range of NATO's nuclear arsenal—but the French position at least meant that France kept in step with the Federal Republic. And France does not want even to hold open the prospect of a third zero in any negotiations over SNF. Earlier, it was Mitterrand who argued in the German Bundestag for deploying cruise and Pershing.

President Bush made the political judgment in 1989 that it was wiser not to press Chancellor Kohl to carry West German public opinion with a decision now to deploy the follow-on to Lance. In managing West German public opinion, it will be helpful if Bush persuades the American Congress to accept that any follow-on to the Lance missile should be developed by the United States on its own authority; in that case, Congress would not make future funding of a Lance replacement dependent on European acceptance of deployment now. Logically, the congressional demand for European support now is reasonable; practically, it is a demand that creates unacceptable strains.

Kohl showed both realism and courage over intermediate-range nuclear forces and the deployment of cruise and Pershing. There is a rational case for some land-based missiles, and if he is still chancellor in a few years, Kohl might well argue for deployments of a follow-on to Lance, one with much longer range. At present, however, he speaks for every significant strand of German opinion in his desire to negotiate to remove some or all SNF missiles on West German territory in return for Soviet reductions.

Collective security demands sensitivity in some countries to the political pressures in others, and so merely lecturing the West Germans on the need for Lance is no solution. If the West German public wants to forgo the full spectrum of nuclear deterrence, that is their government's decision to take. West Germans cannot be forced to deploy missiles on their territory. However, it has been West German leaders, from Konrad Adenauer onward, who have refused to contemplate their country being a conventional battleground, and so urged NATO to threaten nuclear retaliation for any military incursion onto their territory, even if that involved only conventional warfare.

Many politicians familiar with the NATO nuclear planning guidelines have had grave doubts over many years as to whether the political release for firing nuclear artillery, or Lance missiles, would ever be given in the early stages of a conventional attack. Now that the West Germans appear not to want to contemplate such a response, implicitly preferring to rely on aircraft or sea-based nuclear systems, NATO guidelines will change. But the change is not massive, and it need not be damaging.

After all, it was the United States that put forward the zero option, whereby all cruise and Pershing missiles were removed in exchange for the removal of the Soviet SS-20s. It was the United States that overrode its negotiator, Paul Nitze, and rejected the "walk in the woods" formula. Many of us favored Nitze's formulation, for it would have built confidence through reductions while keeping some nuclear missiles on West German territory. By the same logic, Chancellor Kohl and the SACEUR at the time, General Bernard Rodgers, consistently opposed the intermediate-range nuclear forces (INF) treaty and the double zero. They had a point, for NATO had negotiated over the wrong weapon systems first. The weapons NATO could have easily given up were nuclear artillery, and even Lance, if some cruise missile had remained to maintain the nuclear-conventional link.

The American Role

A reduction over a period of years of some of the 325,000 American servicemen on the continent of Europe is inevitable. A cut in the range of 50,000–70,000 troops would be politically manageable for western Europe. There is something to be said for reducing without any formal linkage to CFE, for those talks will take some years to complete. NATO must not budge from its goal of parity nor water down its verification needs because of a wish to cut back quickly to accommodate American budgetary problems. President Bush is entitled to say that he would expect continental western Europe to fill any serious gap left by American forces, any gap that is not taken care of through a CFE agreement. With Spain now a member of the WEU, it should be possible to urge it and France to deploy part of their armed forces forward on the central front in Germany. That in itself might pave the way for the French to provide the commander in chief of all forces in the central front. France's problem with NATO's integrated command structure could be overcome by, for example, keeping the SACEUR an American but having him as an operational commander only for those forces specifically committed by their national government at a time of tension or impending hostilities.

Where President Bush must be careful is in tying American troop levels in Germany to specific weapon systems. Of course, U.S. troops need a credible nuclear component, but to argue that the component *must* be a longer-range follow-on Lance makes it appear that the United States is trying to circumvent the purpose of the INF treaty. What is needed is a complex give and take arrangement that will instill confidence in European-American security cooperation and make Europeans face up to the need to shoulder more responsibility for defense. What is corrosive of confidence is western Europe anxiously awaiting a cutback in American forces and trying to forestall that evil day. Then when the inevitable withdrawal comes, it will create unnecessary ill-will and disruption. Far better to plan now jointly for a different deployment of forces with a maximum transfer of American military technology to Europe. A reduction of U.S. defense spending in Europe is a necessary contribution to correcting the American structural trade deficit. It also happens to be a measure that, compared with protectionism or deflation, carries the least damage to the European Community's own economy.

Assessing Gorbachev

When reappraising East-West relations in the light of Mikhail Gorbachev, it is worth remembering that we in the West are used to describing, and even thinking about, political issues in terms of the personalities of presidents and prime ministers. We do this in part because we have no fundamental divisions over policy issues, and so personality becomes relatively more important. It is too easy to fall into this habit when thinking about the Soviet Union under Gorbachev. But it is a massive mistake to do so, for by concentrating on a commanding personality like his, we divert attention from the historic and continuing policy differences that exist between communist and democratic states. Those differences will remain for many decades, given even the most optimistic assumptions of how fundamental are the developing Soviet reforms.

In contrasting foreign from domestic policy development in the Soviet Union, one finds that the capacity to make very sudden changes in foreign policy predates Mikhail Gorbachev. Stalin, Khrushchev, and even Brezhnev all made sudden changes in foreign policy. Gorbachev is undoubtedly a very charismatic figure, and that helped him convince the Politburo of the need to withdraw from Afghanistan. His carefully orchestrated 1989 meeting in China with its leaders was another big change because he was prepared to meet Chinese conditions for the meeting. He is being constructive in regional international problems—in the Middle East, and over Israel; in central America, even over Nicaragua; and in southern Africa. In foreign affairs, the Politburo has been ready to see Gorbachev make radical changes, and he himself clearly likes being bold in these areas. Yet in truth, foreign policy is relevant to the domestic economy only if the military budget is slashed.

The Soviet attempts to project Gorbachev as a democratic Western-style leader need, however, to be taken with more than a grain of salt. Like any communist leader of his generation, he has an authoritarian past that cannot be sensibly ignored; he is no natural democrat. It has been depressing to see Western news media liken his role as president under the changed Soviet constitution to President Mitterrand's position in the French Republic. All the democratic process and counterchecks present in the French system and absent in the Soviet are forgotten in the urge to present the Gorbachev changes as part of a new, democratic Soviet Union. In fact, the principal checks derive from the fact that, for some time ahead, he will have to carry the Politburo with him, at least in domestic policy. He has not yet developed Stalin's total grip on power.

The Politburo is, as far as we can tell, united in being prepared to take risks with Soviet public opinion to achieve an economically stronger Soviet Union. It also appears ready to respond to Western initiatives with all the Madison Avenue techniques of public relations that have been used so successfully against the Soviets. However, the West underestimates the appalling economic difficulties Mikhail Gorbachev has to overcome and the nature of the doubts within the Politburo, particularly from Ligachev, about how these economic problems are being faced. It is not just a conservative/radical division of opinion; it is also a debate over judgment. Gorbachev's sudden clampdown on alcohol was imperious and ill-considered, and so too, some of his critics feel, is his espousal of glasnost. Glasnost, or more openness, is acceptable inasmuch as it contributes to economic restructuring. Glasnost for its own sake arouses suspicions.

Gorbachev's critics divide from him when they see glasnost introduced not as part of the mechanism for introducing perestroika, but instead as part of a wider pluralist reform package. These critics think the purpose of such reform is unclear and fear it will undermine the authority of the party at the very time when resistance to economic restructuring will be fiercest. To the extent that glasnost feeds nationalist feelings within the Soviet Union, and then leads to a challenge to the integrity of the state, that is an additional cause for concern. By contrast, it can be argued in Gorbachev's favor that without the two sets of reforms' working in tandem, sufficient momentum to force a market economy onto an entrenched authoritarian frame of mind will be lacking. Democracy and market economies go together. But the link may be exaggerated by intellectual advisors in the heady atmosphere close to Gorbachev as they force the pace of change on all fronts.

As yet Gorbachev has given little sign of readiness to cede power on essentials. He and the Politburo are making a clearer definition between overlapping powers of government and party. The authority of government in running day-to-day affairs is being enhanced, and the scope of the party to interfere is being reduced. These are sensible measures, but they should not be misinterpreted. They represent not a dismantling of power but the exercise of power in a different and probably more effective way.

Perestroika has economic reform as its fundamental objective. Yet the substance of economic reform—bringing prices into line with market forces—has barely begun to operate in the Soviet Union. It is hard for us to understand how a sophisticated space program and military machine can be superimposed on such a backward economy. In China, by contrast, the provinces have always yielded real power and a market economy is not an alien concept. The leadership in China has moved far faster than Moscow in accepting markets, decentralizing power and letting the price mechanism operate. But it was very cautious about glasnost, far too cautious for the students. It was the market-governed prices that caused trouble in China, and many fear will unleash comparable disruption in the Soviet Union, but of an even more dangerous sort, kindling nationalism. Yet Soviet leaders have little alternative to price rises if they are to introduce a market economy.

Dissent and disruption have characterized the movement away from Marxist economies in every state that has attempted to introduce market discipline. Poland is a classic example, though it will be interesting to see if the attempt to bind Solidarity into the process of economic reform increases the chance of success. The Soviet Union is unlikely to prove an exception to the rule; discontent over price rises will be considerable. That is why Soviet leaders, including Gorbachev, will hesitate, comforting themselves with the symbols, not the substance, of reform.

To move toward a market economy, Gorbachev will need internal support. Initially, he had no difficulty with the KGB or the armed services over perestroika, but he will have to watch his back when perestroika requires deep cuts in the military budget. In the attempt to reduce Soviet forces in quantity, the generals are demanding offsetting qualitative improvements. Bringing in younger generals means greater flexibility of thought over arms control, but also a greater thirst for the technology of smart weaponry.

One reason there was so little internal resistance initially to perestroika was because it was never the creation just of Gorbachev. In fact, Yuri Andropov started the movement toward reform. Indeed, the reforms had their origin in a debate within the KGB under Andropov in the late 1970s. A reformist wing then began to voice its anxieties about the extent to which the Western democracies were winning the propaganda war with the East.

Those anxieties came to a head over Poland, with the rise and then the suppression of Solidarity. The invasion of Afghanistan ensured that the Soviet Union was jolted by the overt hostility of many Third World countries that had hitherto been regarded as sympathizers. The international section of the KGB sensed the ebbing away of global power as the Soviet economy, which had had some modest growth in the early Brezhnev years, began to stagnate. Those KGB reformists, although they began to advocate change, were then and still are Leninists.

Is Gorbachev a Leninist? Probably. Certainly he makes no major speech inside the Soviet Union without reiterating his commitment to Leninism. Few signs as yet have indicated that he does not mean what he says. Some Western commentators portray his espousal of Leninism as a ritual incantation recited merely to pacify the doubters in the party hierarchy that he is still an orthodox believer. They argue that he is really a pragmatist who wishes only to restore the economic fortunes of the Soviet Union so that it may become once again a complete superpower.

Against this interpretation, however, while Gorbachev's reforms constantly throw up contradictions to conventional Leninism, he appears determined to try to square the circle within the constraints of a pervasive communist ideology Otherwise, how can one explain why new laws make it a crime for a Soviet citizen to have a photocopier or a printer attached to a personal computer? Why is it now easier to declare martial law? Why otherwise do the new laws require special permission to demonstrate?

Most people in the West simply have not recognized this contrast between the rhetoric of glasnost and its actions. Andrei Sakharov, whose own freedom to travel and to criticize is itself a welcome aspect of glasnost, was right to draw attention to the new concentration of power in recent Soviet laws. These laws are being introduced at the very time when the widespread perception in the West is that the Soviet Union is making a concerted movement toward decentralization and pluralism. How can perceptions differ so much? One reason is that while newspaper reports concentrate on speeches, most Soviet citizens are still awaiting the implementation of the promises of those speeches. Soviet intellectuals are enthusiastic about their freedom to criticize, to expose the excesses of the Stalinist era, and, even more recently to criticize Brezhnev. For them life in Russia is vastly improved. But their enthusiasm does not yet mean much in the lives of the great majority of the Soviet citizens. Leon Trotsky is being rehabilitated in the pages of *Pravda*, but that is far removed for most people from their daily life of shortages and pettifogging bureaucracy.

The West needs to develop a greater measure of skepticism over glasnost's true democratic credentials. Many Western politicians and media commentators are fascinated by the new changes in and of themselves; moreover, the pace of change makes any appraisal soon out of date. For example, even as skeptical and farsighted a commentator on Soviet affairs as Leonard Schapiro wrote in 1974, "The rehabilitation of Bukharin may come—who can tell? If it ever does, it will be a sure sign that real and substantial changes have taken place in the essential nature of the Soviet system of rule." Now that Bukharin's rehabilitation is under way, it has to be taken very seriously as a landmark reform. Yet, for all that, caution is still in order about what might be possible. No one can predict the future with any confidence. We are watching a revolution, and it can go any of a number of ways.

The Imperative of Economics

In avoiding the trap of rather naive conventional wisdom about Gorbachev, we must, above all, not lose sight of the economic imperative behind all his reforms. Those who hold out against current fashion by criticizing the nature of the democratic reforms and refusing to pass quickly over the far less newsworthy failure of the economic reforms are right to raise such questions. When they doubt the reality of the economic reforms, they are inevitably depicted as reactionary, and as wishing to perpetuate the cold war, but skepticism is needed.

It is unfashionable these days even to mention Soviet propaganda. Yet propaganda has been an essential part of Soviet power since Lenin. Propaganda remains vital to this day. What is different about Gorbachev's propaganda is its quality and sophistication. And troubling signs suggest that it is succeeding in inducing the West to misread Soviet priorities. We are falling too easily into the trap of believing what we want to believe—namely, that the Soviet Union has abandoned any wish to be a dominating power in the world, and that if it proceeds to rebuild its economy, it will be content to use its new economic power benignly.

The Soviet Union and the countries of the Warsaw Pact are going to pass through a delicate transition. Prudence dictates a careful, consistent, and united approach to our security during this period. History shows that governments encountering internal difficulties often seek to divert attention from those difficulties by raising the specter of external danger to maintain morale at home.

The West would be far wiser to respond to the challenge that the language of Gorbachev's reforms represents by giving greater weight to his actions. Since he calls himself a Leninist, why should we not accept him at his word and guard against the day when he may wish to exercise a dominating role? We should rid ourselves of the assumption that he is a closet democrat longing to introduce a liberal democratic society. His Leninism may become only skin deep; perhaps we are witnessing a political transformation. If so, he will eventually abandon Lenin's dream of worldwide ideological influence. But let us welcome that day when it comes. It has not yet arrived. As the Soviet economy fails to make what it wants, the temptation to take what it wants will grow.

Meanwhile, we should watch carefully the divisions happening inside the Soviet Union. It was General de Gaulle who warned "Russia holds a dozen Algerias within her borders." In Georgia and Armenia, as well as in Azerbaijan, the authority of the communist party has been brutally asserted over the nationalists. Gorbachev knows that nationalism represents a deeply sensitive political challenge to his authority. He knows that each of the trouble spots is different. How the Armenian situation develops matters, though it may not have a profound effect on the situation in Estonia, Latvia, and Lithuania, let alone the Muslim republics. Yet if Moscow's authority is challenged, it would be out of character for the communist party not to assert its authority and resist fissiparous nationalist tendencies by force.

The calculation that Europe and the United States have to make, and in part already have made, is a hard-headed one. To what extent is it worth helping to build up Soviet economic strength, which could in turn buttress military strength? To what extent should we encourage Moscow to cut its staggeringly high defense budget by reducing our own defense spending? To what extent is it realistic to hope that economic liberalism and market forces will sow the seeds of political pluralism and an eventual movement toward democracy? The Western democracies are having to make nothing less than a calculated gamble, for freeing up trade and credit to the Soviet Union will no doubt provide it room it could use to reequip a trimmed-down armed forces.

The Federal Republic has made the choice to a greater extent than most realize. That is illustrated by the joint exploitation of the mineral resources in the Kola peninsula; by the DM 3 billion Deutsche Bank credit to fund capital investment in the food and consumer goods industries; by the building of the thermal reactor as a joint venture in Dmitrovgrad; and by Lufthansa's agreement to modernize Moscow's four airports. In all, some 200 Soviet-West German joint ventures have already been formed, while France, Japan, and the United States in combination have not quite a fifth as many.

The continuing buildup of Soviet military strength poses an ever-present anxiety for NATO. New tanks continue to roll off the assembly line no more slowly under Gorbachev than they did under his predecessors. Large nuclear-powered submarines move down the slipways just as frequently. Only when these lines visibly slow will we know that the Soviet Union is really matching action to rhetoric.

These uncomfortable facts should raise question marks that must not be obscured by the signing of the INF treaty, or abandoned with a successful strategic arms treaty, or dropped because Mikhail Gorbachev announces successive cuts of tanks, missiles, and men in the Soviet armed forces—welcome though those are. We need to question whether the tanks that are being withdrawn are not just older T-55s and T-62s, but the modern T-80s, T-64Bs, and T-72Ms; whether Russian troops that are to be demobilized are not just Asiatic troops who are unable to speak Russian and whose loyalty can not be guaranteed; whether the river-bridging offensive equipment is not just withdrawn but dismantled; whether the nature of Soviet military exercises changes from offensive to purely defensive; and whether the missiles that go are simply those that the military itself no longer wants.

Taking the Gamble

On the side of the West's choosing to be generous with economic and technological change is the clear evidence of a far greater openness and new thinking in the Soviet Union than ever existed in the Khrushchev reform years. It is also becoming ever clearer that while perestroika started with purely economic objectives, and glasnost was initially seen as part of economic reform, glasnost has developed in Gorbachev's mind, and in that of his foreign minister, Edvard Shevardnadze, a momentum of its own.

Glasnost is also triggering important reforms within the communist world. The picture in China, North Korea, Vietnam, and eastern Europe is mixed. Hungary appears to be the country most genuinely trying to create political pluralism. Czechoslovakia allowed Dubcek, its formerly disgraced leader, to travel to Italy, but when he criticized the government, he found himself once again confined to his home territory. In Poland, General Jaruzelski makes much of his friendship with Gorbachev and has negotiated an important agreement with Solidarity. Yet he clipped the union's wings with the closure of Gdansk shipyards, and one is left wondering whether his undoubted nationalism is not just covering a sophisticated suppression of Solidarity. Nevertheless, in eastern Europe, nationalism follows national boundaries, and it becomes ever harder for the Soviet Union to stop a true democracy from emerging in these countries. Perhaps the Soviet Union has stopped even trying.

Maybe Soviet tanks will never roll through central European cities again, as they did in Hungary in 1956 and Czechoslovakia in 1968. Even Brezhnev held back from deploying tanks in Poland in 1980. Instead, Moscow concentrated on stiffening the Polish army to exert control through martial law. This was a new development within communism—allowing the Polish army to exert more power than the party. It is noticeable how powerful the army has become in eastern Europe; in the Soviet Union itself under Brezhnev, the party's previous scrupulous arms-length relationship with the army ended. It has been interesting to see how the Soviet army accepted the withdrawal from Afghanistan and managed to put the politicians on the rack of public opinion for going in the first place, while escaping any public criticism for its failure. The army is becoming the most interesting political factor in the Soviet Union.

In East Germany, it looks as if the reformist route will have to await a new generation of leaders. East Germany has benefited economically from the Treaty of Rome's exceptional provision that West and East Germany can be treated for trade purposes as one. Yet East Germany has been remarkably resistant to reforms, which have not yet followed prosperity. Without a very determined strategy for linking political freedom with economic concessions, the communist party will retain its grip. Meanwhile, the Federal Republic has concentrated, naturally enough, on negotiating to reunite German families.

Overall, the pace of change inside eastern Europe was slower until Gorbachev took over than many anticipated. The region's human rights record has been patchy. The situation in Romania has deteriorated fast, and no one has seemed able to stop it. As part of the Helsinki Final Act, the Western nations decided to coordinate their handling of the Soviet Union in both NATO and the European Community. Those same mechanisms need to be used again. To some of us it seemed a mistake to agree in principle to a human rights conference in Moscow, and the West should establish yardsticks—for the release of political prisoners and other human rights issues—and make it clear that unless these conditions are met, a decision not to go to Moscow is possible. Alas, it is hard to escape the conclusion that the die is already cast and the West will attend at Moscow, boosting Gorbachev's limited definition of human rights.

Finally, the clinching argument for the West's taking the risk and helping the Soviet economy is that the Politburo just may have let a democratic genie out of the bottle that cannot be put back. Certainly it cannot be put back without reversing course and heightening repression. But repression's history is too recent for us to pretend that it cannot return. What the West needs is patience, an attitude in short supply in politics.

The West has an opportunity to influence Soviet development, but we should not exaggerate that influence. It is, nevertheless, an opportunity that might not recur for decades. If we are to take the gamble and make available both sensitive technology and money on preferential terms, common prudence dictates that we attach strings to such actions. The best strings are clear milestones toward a genuine market. By contrast, supporting continued subsidies and protectionism within the Soviet Union will only waste this opportunity. So far the manner in which Europe is pursuing Soviet trading opportunities offers little room for confidence that we can agree and hold to such milestones.

We are competing against each other, not just for trade but also for favors. The Soviet leadership must be cynically amused to see our leaders compete for television and photo opportunities in Red Square. Western banks are tripping over themselves to lend at preferential rates. It is by no means clear that we have learned the lessons of Norway's folly in letting the Soviet navy into the priceless secret of Western submarine propeller technology. All signs indicate that without greater self-discipline, serious military secrets will be transferred at minimal cost. This indulgent incontinence from the West must delight the KGB and cause anguish to the Central Intelligence Agency.

It is vital that both the OECD and the NATO nations try to establish agreed guidelines. Some countries argue that it is not worth the effort. They hold that the guidelines will be broken and different national perceptions will make it impossible to reach agreement. They point to the fruitless row between the United States and Europe over the Soviet gas pipeline in the early 1980s. Admittedly, the task will be difficult. The alternative, however, is not only division but chaos, which will offer the Soviet Union major opportunities and fuel American fears of European Community protectionism accompanying the internal market in 1992.

If the economic restructuring of perestroika turns out to be far, far slower than Gorbachev imagines, if it brings in its wake consumer dissatisfaction and feeds nationalist fervor in the Soviet Union, who can be sure that East-West relations will remain on their present harmonious course even over trade? The Soviet Union presents a market of nearly 300 million people, cheap labor, land, and raw materials. But the obstacles to freer trade are many, especially the nonconvertibility of the ruble. Soviet leaders talk of easing controls and then having full convertibility within the decade. That is a very ambitious target, but one to which the West should attempt to hold the Soviet Union as part of the responsibility of membership in the World Bank and the International Monetary Fund.

We do not have much influence on Soviet internal reforms, but we have an indirect influence. Publicly announced yardsticks for foreign behavior will provide some rough guide to the progress of internal reform. For instance, the repatriation of profits by joint venture companies has been a recurring problem. Now, profits can be paid in the investor's own currency, but with a 20 percent tax designed to encourage reinvestment. In this area, too, it is worth the West's trying to agree to time scales over which such restrictions will be lifted.

In all of these areas the European Community has the opportunity for leadership. A demanding, disciplined relationship with the Soviet Union from the outset is the only way to stimulate real, rather than rhetorical, reforms. For President Bush, the challenge is to encourage Gorbachev to continue with asymmetrical cuts in Soviet armed forces and equipment. That will require a clear sense of America's security relations with Europe, one that can be set only with the frankness in NATO that friendship requires. To encourage economic reform in the Soviet Union in the hope that it will foster a democratic revolution is acceptable; to fail to reinsure during that revolution is totally unacceptable. Revolutions are notorious for being harbingers of insecurity. We must safeguard our security now with as much vigilance as before the Gorbachev reforms, indeed, perhaps more. But we must also respond positively to Soviet military reductions. It is a delicate balance to strike.

Advisory Group:
Project on European-American Relations

Cyrus R. Vance, Chairman
Robert D. Hormats, Vice Chairman
Gregory F. Treverton, Director of Project
Steven J. Monde, Assistant to the Director

David Aaron
George W. Ball
Seweryn Bialer
John Brademas
Hodding Carter, III
Robert F. Ellsworth
Murray H. Finley
Richard N. Gardner
Stanley Hoffmann
Robert E. Hunter
Irving Kristol
Jan M. Lodal
Charles S. Maier
Robert S. McNamara
Harald B. Malmgren
Maynard Parker
William R. Pearce

Robert V. Roosa
Nathaniel Samuels
J. Robert Schaetzel
John W. Seigle
Marshall D. Shulman
Robert B. Silvers
Anthony M. Solomon
Helmut Sonnenfeldt
Joan E. Spero
Ronald Steel
Fritz Stern
John R. Stevenson
John H. Watts, III

Nicholas X. Rizopoulos, *ex officio*
Peter Tarnoff, *ex officio*

About the Authors

Gregory F. Treverton is Senior Fellow at the Council on Foreign Relations with responsibility for European and politico-military issues, and the Director of the European-American Project. He has worked in the U.S. government on the staff of the first Senate Select Committee on Intelligence (the Church Committee) and as staff member for Western Europe on the National Security Council during the Carter administration. He was Director of Studies at the International Institute for Strategic Studies in London, and immediately before joining the Council, was for six years a faculty member of the John F. Kennedy School of Government at Harvard. He is the author of *The "Dollar Drain" and American Forces in Germany, Nuclear Weapons in Europe, Making the Alliance Work: The United States and Western Europe,* and, most recently, *Covert Action: The Limits of Intervention in the Postwar World.*

Pierre Hassner is Research Director at the Centre d'Etudes et de Recherches Internationales, Foundation Nationale des Science Politiques in Paris. He is the author of numerous works in French and English, including contributions to Sarah Meiklejohn Terry, editor, *Soviet Policy In Easter Europe,* Lincoln Gordon, editor, *Eroding Empire,* and Michael Mandelbaum, editor, *Western Approaches to the Soviet Union.*

David P. Calleo is Professor and Director of European Studies at Johns Hopkins Paul H. Nitze School of Advanced International Studies. He is a regular contributor to scholarly journals and the author of many books, including, *The Imperious Economy* and, most recently, *Beyond American Hegemony.*

Robert D. Hormats is Vice Chairman of Goldman Sachs International Corporation. He has served in the U.S. government as Assistant Secretary of State for Economic and Business Affairs from 1981 to 1982; as Deputy Trade Representative from 1979 to

1981; and as Deputy Assistant Secretary of State for Economic and Business Affairs from 1977 to 1979. Previously, Mr. Hormats was a Senior Staff Member for International Economic Affairs on the National Security Council from 1974 to 1977. In addition he was a member of the U.S. delegation to the Versailles, Ottawa, and Venice economic summits.

Johan Jørgen Holst is Norwegian Minister of Defense. Previously, he served the Norwegian government as State Secretary of the Ministry of Defense from 1976 to 1979, and from 1979 to 1981 as State Secretary of the Ministry of Foreign Affairs. In the private sector, he has served as the Head of Research, and later as Director, at the Institution for International Affairs.

Richard N. Perle is Resident Scholar at the American Enterprise Institute and contributing editor of *U.S. News and World Report.* From 1981 until 1987, he held the post of Assistant Secretary of Defense for International Security Policy. In that capacity he served as Chairman of NATO's High Level Group and head of the American delegation to the Risk Reduction Negotiations with the Soviet Union. Prior to assuming office at the Pentagon, he spent the years between 1969 and 1980 on the staff of the Senate Committee on Government Operations, the Committee on Armed Services, the Arms Control Subcommittee, and on the personal staff of Senator Henry Jackson.

David Owen, a member of Parliament, is co-founder and leader of the the British Social Democratic Party. He served as Secretary of State for Foreign and Commonwealth Affairs from 1977 to 1979 and as Opposition Spokesman for Energy from 1979 to 1980. After co-founding the S.D.P in 1981 he was Chairman of the Parliamentary Committee from 1981 to 1982 and Deputy Leader of the S.D.P. from 1982 to 1983.